COLORADO'S
LOST
GOLDMINES
AND
BURRIED
TREASURE

T0159241

Colorado's LOST GOLDMINES & BURIED TREASURE

CAROLINE BANCROFT

assisted by AGNES NAFZIGER

BOWER HOUSE

DENVER

BowerHouseBooks.com

Cover Design and Illustration by Margaret McCullough

Library of Congress Cataloging-inPublication Data on file.

About the Author

Caroline Bancroft is a third generation Coloradan who began writing her first history for *The Denver Post* in 1928. Her long-standing interest in western history was inherited. Her pioneer grandfather, Dr. F. J. Bancroft, was a founder of the Colorado Historical Society and its first president. His granddaughter has carried on the family tradition. She is the author of the interesting series of Bancroft Books, *Silver Queen: The Fabulous Story of Baby Doe Tabor, Famous Aspen, Denver's Lively Past, Historic Central City, The Brown Palace in Denver, Tabor's Matchless Mine and Lusty Leadville, Augusta Tabor: Her Side of the Scandal, The Unsinkable Mrs. Brown, Unique Ghost Towns and Mountain Spots,* and *Colorful Colorado.*

A Bachelor of Arts from Smith College, she later obtained a Master of Arts degree from the University of Denver, writing her thesis on Central City, Colorado. Her full-size *Gulch of Gold* is the definitive and attractive history of that well-known area and has attained wide popularity through the many visitors to the annual Central City Opera and Play Festival.

Miss Bancroft is shown with Agnes Nafziger in a photograph taken in 1961 by Daniel K. Peterson at Mrs. Nafziger's home in Central City.

STEPHEN L. R. McNCHOLS
Governor of Colorado
1957-1963

Contents

(See the Colorado Map on the Next Page for Locations)

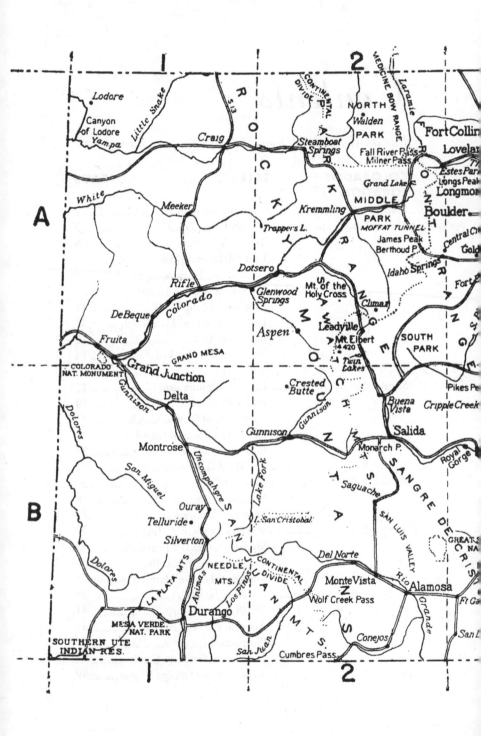

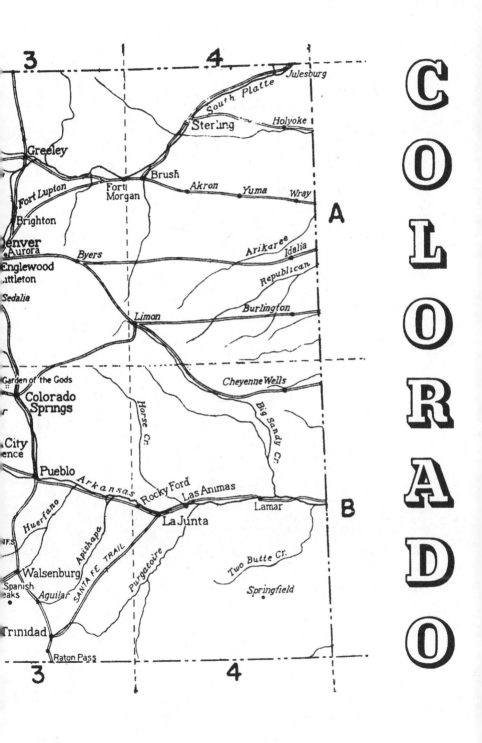

Personal to the Reader

My father, George Jarvis Bancroft, was a consulting engineer. He held degrees both in mining and in civil engineering, particularly reclamation of the latter division. In the early 1900's he was very successful, and his fees more than sustained a living for his young wife and two daughters.

But the Panic of 1907 caused a number of his Eastern clients to withdraw both their interest and their investments in the West. He found it harder and harder to make a living at his chosen profession, especially as Colorado mining became slower and more restricted. By 1913 the family finances were a matter for real concern.

Father decided to accept a regular job and became editor of the *Mining and Industrial* page of the *Rocky Mountain News*, a page crammed with hard facts and my father's brilliant reports.

In 1914 he decided to try to liven the page with human interest, and he thought of the idea of running Lost Mine stories. Naturally he knew dozens, as he had mined throughout the West, Mexico and Australia. One of the new department's most avid readers was the editor's sixth-grade daughter, Caroline.

Many year later, in 1929, when I was editor of a literary page on *The Denver Post*, I thought I would like to write a book about the West. I remembered Father's Lost Mine stories and started to collect them on my own. But the next year J. Frank Dobie published *Coronado's Children*, an immediate best-seller. I decided I had been scooped.

Yet my interest in folklore continued. From 1941 through 1955 I was one of the sponsors for the Western Folklore Conference, headed by Levette J. Davidson and held each July on the University of Denver campus. Every summer I gave a paper on some phase of Colorado folklore.

One of my papers was *Lost Mine Legends of Colorado*. It was read during the summer of 1943 and published the following October in the *California* (now Western) *Folklore Quarterly*. As a scholarly resume of the subject, this article still stands alone, and I recommend a reading at the library for anyone interested in a detached approach.

What is offered here in this booklet is the credulous point of view, a culling of thirty of my collection, told as they might be around a campfire for entertainment's sake. I have been assisted in the writing by Agnes Nafziger, short story writer with many years of training in the narrative technique.

We hope they divert you as much as they entertained us while preparing the stories for publication.

Caroline Bancroft
President, 1955-61
Colorado Folklore Society

(See Frontispiece Map for Location)

Unprofitable Murder

Long after the ancient Uintah Indian had shuffled off to his pile of blankets in the back of the General Store, Pete Madison sat on a nail keg, going over the story the old man had told him. Pete's bones ached; he had come in at sundown from a prospecting trip in the Pat's Hole section of Moffat County. It was a hard ride—ten long hours on a back-jolting mule while Pete pulled a pack burro plodding behind. He planned to bed down after a couple of warming drinks and a good hot meal. But the old Indian next to him at the bar had started talking, and his story drove all ideas of food and sleep from Pete's mind. As the old Indian turned to leave, Pete followed him, asking if that was all he had to say.

"All," the Indian said. "Nobody ever find mine. It is there. Gold does not change. It does not rot. Gold is still there. You find it."

He turned in at the General Store where he slept and refused to say more. The owner of the store, coming back from supper, suggested that Pete leave—he wanted to close up.

"You think the old man's story of the lost gold mine here in Moffat County has anything to it?" Pete asked.

The storekeeper shrugged. "Why don't you talk to Harry Chew, rancher a few miles out? They say he knows a few things about it."

Pete went to bed—it was too late tonight to find Harry Chew. He thought again about the story of the two brothers. Red and Eli Hanson had worked off by themselves through a bitter stormy winter at the end of which they had twenty-five pounds of gold. Being short of supplies and feeling the need of a little celebration, they headed out of the canyon for a nearby settlement. Just across the Utah line, they were attacked by six gunmen.

It was a lost battle from the first—the two prospectors, gaunt and weary from a long winter of privation and work, against half a dozen husky desperadoes. The men had been lying in wait for miners with the gold dug out the past months. Red and Eli, their backs to an over-hanging ledge of granite and earth, were downed by bullets.

The outlaws eagerly searched the bodies, the saddle-bags of the horses and the pack on the burro's back. They found barely enough gold to pay for supplies and a small spree in town.

For this bit of gold, they stood in danger of hanging—if the miners' deaths were discovered. To stall off any discovery of the killing, they pried off the face of the ledge and covered the bodies with rock and dirt.

Where was the rich mine Red and Eli had left? Where was the rest of the gold, no doubt safely hidden while they went to town?

Questions to make Pete's mind reel with golden phantoms, luring him through dim distances, tangled canyons and down endless mountain slopes. The clink of gold chimed above the noisy barrage of outlaw bullets and the silenced voices of the two who had struck it rich in secret, and kept their secret in death.

Pete was up before dawn and on his way to Harry Chew, old-time rancher. When Pete asked him about the Indian's story, Chew sighed.

"Son, if that story gets out, this country will be crawling with treasure-hunters, come snow-melting time. If you can keep it under your hat, I'll tell you what I found, and what makes me dead sure that somewhere up in them gulches is a pile of gold just waiting to be picked up. Some years ago before the rheumatiz got me, I was exploring a steep cliff over in Pool Canyon—that's right across the line in Utah. I saw an odd-shaped rock at the foot of the ledge, and, when I picked it up, it was a human skull. Wondering if there was more than just a skull, I dug around."

Pete waited while the old rancher filled his pipe, wrinkle-lidded eyes musing. "I found two bodies, son. Two bodies, and on one skull was a bit of hair, red as fire. Right away I thought of the Hanson boys, who had disappeared. The last time I saw them I'd ridden out after a mountain cat that had been killing my calves, and I came across the boys cooking their chow. They warn't friendly, but I knew they was the Hanson brothers, who'd been prospecting around here for a couple of years. Nobody ever heard of them after the time I saw them."

"The Indian said a bunch of outlaws attacked and shot them," Pete put in. "Where'd he get that?"

"Years later, a rip-roaring drunk was bragging about seeing two fellows shot down—and not enough gold on 'em to pay for the bullets." Then Chew said, in the words of the Uintah Indian, "Gold does not change. It does not rot. The gold is still there. Maybe you find it."

Pete Madison tried. He even talked old Harry Chew into climbing on a horse and leading the way up the winding gulches. They found empty prospector holes, shallow shafts with no sign of pay dirt, caves where wild animals made their home. They even found rusted picks, a weathered mound that might cover twenty-five pounds of hidden gold.

But they found no gold. They found no rich mine.

It is there—somewhere. For as the old Indian said, gold does not change, nor rot. It is there—and someone, maybe, will yet find it.

Also told by Editha Watson in the *Herald Democrat* (Leadville), 1935

Caught by the Glitter

The glitter of gold can often fool the wide-eyed tenderfoot, and even, sometimes, the hardened Westerner. It happened—or did it?—to Owen Thom, prominent feed merchant and lumber dealer of Aspen, back in 1899.

On a bright June morning in that buzzing silver town, Thom was just opening the doors of his store, when in walked a tall, gangly fellow of nineteen or so. He had an earnest, freckled face from which clear blue eyes looked up in an appealing way to the older man.

"Young kid out here alone, and kind of scared," Thom thought, his heart warming.

In the comfort of their eastern homes, so many of them hearing about the quick fortunes and red-blooded adventure of the West, started out, hopes wild and sky-high—only to find loneliness and starvation, even death. This kid, Thom decided, was one of them. Didn't look like a tramp. He must have come from a good home and wasn't tough enough to make good in a two-fisted country.

"Can I help you, young man?" Thom asked with a cordiality meant to show the young fellow he had come to the right place. "Looks like you been traveling some."

The boy's grin was wide and winsome. "I have, sir. I came from Meeker, where I had a herd of horses, but the Indians stole them. Was no work for me there, so I walked all the way to Aspen, hoping I'd find a job."

"Tried anywhere else?" Thom asked. The kid had spunk, that was sure. Had a clean-cut look too, despite the worn clothes and dust-crusted boots.

"I tried several places," the boy admitted, "but I like the looks of your place. I wish, sir, you had a job for me."

Thom beamed. He was proud of his prosperous establishment. "Well, now, just mebbe I have. Bet you want some breakfast first off, however. Got any money?"

The boy's freckled face flushed. "No sir, but I got—this." He drew a rock from his pocket. "I don't know much about mining, but the gold specks in this—are they really gold, or copper?"

Owen Thom, hardened by seeing rich ore many a time in the fabulous silver camp of Aspen, felt his eyes bulge. The boy's rock, a piece of quartz, was crawling with free gold. Thom swallowed. "Where —where'd you get that?" he blurted.

THE ELK MOUNTAINS SECRETE LOST MINES

"Oh, I stopped to sleep the other night about ten miles out of town, I think. You see, I was heading up the Roaring Fork for Independence. But I turned back ten miles out and decided to return to Aspen. On a big cliff where I bedded down, I saw this pretty stone sticking out of a slab. The way the sun, just setting, was shining on it, it looked like copper a-blazing."

"Well." Thom's voice was husky in the effort to restrain his excitement. A piece of ore like this could mean one of the richest strikes in the country! "Looks interesting, son, but why don't you leave it with me, and I'll have it assayed? If it's any good, you and me will go partners and mine that place. Sure you remember where you got it?"

"Sure I remember." The boy looked a little surprised. "I could walk right back to it this minute, only—" he grinned engagingly— "I'm hungry."

"Don't you worry. I'll fix that, son," Thom said gruffly. He went to his cash drawer and got some gold coins. "Now you go get a room first in that hotel on the corner—best hotel in town. Get yourself all cleaned up—looks like you could use another pair of boots—"

The boy flushed again. "I been walking a long ways, sir."

Thom got another ten-dollar gold piece from the drawer. "Buy some new boots, son. Take today to rest up—fill up that skinny body of yours, get to bed early and come back here by seven in the morning. You can work for me till we get our mine to rolling!"

The boy let out a breath, seemed about to say something, but instead hurried off, stuffing the gold coins in his pocket. As Thom, the gold-studded quartz in his hand, watched the skinny young fellow go down the street, he realized he had not even asked the boy's name. His glance came back to the specimen, its flecks of gold glinting in the sun. Reckon the rock was as good as a name. Should run $40,000 to the ton.

At seven next morning, Thom was waiting for the young man. Seven-thirty, and he had not arrived. Eight. Eight-thirty. Well, he had probably had himself a big time yesterday, buying new clothes, eating high on the hog, and sleeping it off in a soft, clean hotel bed. Give the lad time. He would show up.

But he never did show up. He had shopped, eaten and stayed at the Hotel Jerome—on Thom's money. Then he disappeared. Many people remembered him around town—a starry-eyed freckled young kid, happy and excited with gold coins jingling in his levis. They never saw him again.

Thom had the specimen. It was as rich as he had judged. But where had it come from? Had the boy really picked it from an outcropping on a ledge, ten miles or so on the way to Independence?

Thom and his friends talked it over. Thom believed the boy was honest—and innocent. He just did not know what the specimen was worth, nor what it portended. Others claim Thom had been gypped. All the boy wanted was free lodging and food, and now he was pulling the same trick with another good-looking specimen that he had stolen from some paying mine, on some other nice fatherly man like Thom.

But every single one made a secret note in his mind about a spot some ten miles east on the trail to Independence, where a slab stuck out of a high ledge. When the sun shone on it, it blazed like copper— or gold.

To date, no such spot has been discovered. It may be there—it may not. But many people still figure it pays to look for it.

Also told by the *Denver Times*, 1899

Trapper's Treasure

Back in the early 1860's, Trapper Sam made many trips into Denver, bringing with him the skins he had trapped up around Breckenridge. This was nothing unusual. But he also brought with him gold, lots of gold, and he had a strange hobby—carving small wooden spades by the dozen.

As he carved, he talked freely of the best place to trap beaver, mountain cats and bear. But he turned as mute as one of his wooden spades when his gold was mentioned. Where he got gold was his secret, and his alone.

The spades were big enough to shovel the snow from the doorstep of his cabin. They were all alike—same size, smoothly shaved, the long handle curved at the top and the spade part hollowed out like a frying pan.

One winter Trapper Sam did not show up. There was wondering and guessing by his cronies down on 15th street, where he had had the same room year after year. It was decided he died a natural death up in the mountain wilderness he loved.

If only he had told somebody what mine kept producing such rich ore for him all these years! Prospectors up in Breckenridge had not found out anything either, and they were plenty curious. Although rich finds were common in the area, it was unusual for a man to keep a strike as rich as Trapper Sam's a tight secret.

The mine's whereabouts seemed doomed to die with Sam. He was all but forgotten when one day in the 1890's, a miner called Zeb, prospecting far up near timberline above Breckenridge, saw an old tumbledown cabin to one side of a mine dump. Inside the cabin was nothing but an old plank cot and table. Zeb climbed up on the dump, and at the mouth of the tunnel were three rusty shovels, shaped like a frying pan. The curved handles were weathered and storm-bitten, but whole.

Zeb stepped inside the tunnel. Here was another spade, but more interesting to the prospector was the black, talc-like ore on the tunnel walls. He had never seen anything like it. With his hammer he knocked off several specimens. Having nothing with him to carry them in, he emptied his tobacco-sack and used it for the ore. He took one of the spades and started for Breckenridge, anxious to learn what the strange black ore could be. In his hurry, he did not watch for signs, and got lost. A couple of days later he finally staggered into town. An old-timer, seeing the spade, remembered Sam the Trapper.

"And you found his mine!" the oldster cried unbelievingly.

"That I did. Here's some rocks from it, right in my tobacco-sack." He reached a hand in his pocket.

"Funny," he said blankly. "Has to be this pocket—only one with no holes in it. Dad-rat it, it's gone. Reckon I dropped it climbing down. Well, we'll go back and get some more."

The two miners lost no time in tramping back up the gulches, Zeb strutting ahead confidently. His confidence oozed away when no matter which trail he took, it did not lead to the old cabin with the spades. Crestfallen, Zeb promised his friend he would keep looking till he found it.

"If you didn't have the spade, I'd say you made up the whole story," his friend muttered. "But nobody else made spades like that."

The two continued searching for years—to no avail—they never found the place.

The old-timers claim Trapper Sam reached out a ghostly hand and took that tobacco-sack of ore from Zeb's pocket. Then he turned Zeb's mind around so Zeb was too confused to know where he had been or where he was going. Trapper Sam did not want anybody to have his mine, and he was watching over it in death as closely as he had in life.

Whatever the explanation, the truth is that to this day nobody has been able to find the old cabin with the spades, nor the mine with its black, talc-like ore.

Also told by Editha L. Watson in the *Herald Democrat* (Leadville) 1935

Lost Pitchblende Mine

Although gold holds the most magic and glamorous lure, there are other ores as rich. One story of Colorado lost mines concerns a metal that was once considered worthless, but is now extremely valuable—pitchblende. Pitchblende ore contains uranium.

Roscoe Morton of Idaho Springs told of the time in the early 1900's when two carloads—forty tons—of pitchblende ore were shipped from the Jo Reynolds mine to the Argo Smelter. The miners were paid only for the gold content—nothing for worthless pitchblende.

However, this shipment was of such high grade that it attracted the national attention of mineralogists, and specimens were saved for mineral collections. The *Georgetown Courier* wrote quite a story about it, which was copied by many newspaper across the country.

When pitchblende became valuable through scientific achievements of Marie and Pierre Curie in isolating radium, Morton remembered that high-grade shipment. He decided to investigate the Reynolds mine, well-known to him, where the ore had come from.

It was no problem to find the Reynolds mine. But all he was able to find were some handsome geraniums blooming around the shaft-house. And neither mineral expert nor old-time prospector with his uncanny, intuitive feel for pay ore, has been able to find anywhere in the Reynolds mine the vein that carries the metal now so valuable.

Also told by George Jarvis Bancroft in the *Rocky Mountain News*, 1914

Grand Lake Treasure

A silver-handled hunting knife in an ancient, towering spruce on the eastern shore of Grand Lake points to the hiding-place of an old iron Dutch oven. In the oven is a fortune in gold dust.

It was hidden there in the 1850's by a group of men who had struck it rich in California in the gold rush of '49. Returning East to enjoy and share their wealth with their families, they were attacked by Ute Indians near the present town of Steamboat Springs. Only four of the group managed to elude the hostile redskins. They made their way to Grand Lake where they camped for several days, resting from their ordeal, hunting and fishing.

The Indian attack made them realize what a dangerous trip lay ahead, not only Indian enemies but also blizzards, floods, outlaws. The precious gold dust had become a burden. After serious consultation they decided to hide most of their wealth near the lake, go home and return in the spring. Then they would come better equipped to carry such an important burden across the perilous plains.

Their heavy Dutch oven was ideal to hold the gold. A spot to bury it was chosen near a huge gray boulder, shaped like a giant tombstone, on the east shore of the wide lake. A rock such as this was too big to be dislodged by any storm waves of the high mountain waters and too sturdy to be broken by ice packs tossed against it in the bitter winter near the Continental Divide. It would be an indestructible marker for the owners, when they returned in the spring for their treasure.

One of the men was doubtful. He pointed to the many vast boulders tossed about in prehistoric times that lined the lake on all sides. Supposing—through the winter—their image of this particular rock was dulled by distance. Suppose they came back several months hence, only to see rock after rock after rock—this one it was, no, that one—no, this one.

More than a stone marker was needed.

"I'll take my knife," he said, drawing it from his belt, "and drive it to the hilt in this tree. See—its shadow by the morning sun falls on our rock."

The bright mountain sun sparkled on the silver handle for a moment before the speaker thrust his knife into the trunk of the spruce, where thick branches hid it from the casual observer.

The four men set out across the range, and made it safely to the plains. There they were again attacked by Indians, and this time three of them were killed. The lone survivor eventually reached home.

But weakened by the strenuous journey, he knew death was near, and told his family of the silver knife in the spruce beside the mountain lake.

In the spring searchers, organized by his family, were unable to find the tree with the knife nor any trace of a grave containing an iron oven. They found many big boulders shaped like a giant tombstone. Finally they gave up.

Others on down through the years have taken up the search with no success. The trail to Adams Falls passes right by where the treasure ought to be. One party, returning after several years for still one more try, was appalled to find the gigantic machinery of the Colorado-Big Thompson reclamation project uprooting part of the forest on the east shore to level the ground.

Was the tree with the silver hunting-knife uprooted by a bulldozer?

Or did that tree with its golden-treasure marker escape and grow tall, and thicker and thicker, burying the knife?

There are those who say that on a moonlit night, something deep in a mighty old spruce, towering among its brother trees on the shore of a wide mountain lake, gleams and glitters, almost like a luminescent hand beckoning from the dark stiff-needled branches.

Or is it an ancient silver-handled hunting-knife, timelessly pointing to an old iron oven, buried at its feet?

So far the ghostly gleam has been only that—unreal, a phantom star. But it could happen—when the sun's glittering rays are just right, or the moon's glow pierces the branches to the trunk in the right spot—that someone may see the old hunting-knife and know he is close to the buried treasure.

Also told by Mary L. Cairns in *The Olden Days*, 1954

Snowslide on Slate Mountain

In October, 1879, Buck Rogers was one of thirty wildly excited men who struck it rich on Slate Mountain, near Red Cliff. As usual Buck celebrated by getting drunk on Taos Lightning. One hundred thousand dollars in gold ore—and more to come! A whole mountain of gold, just waiting to be blasted out! It was enough to make a man drunk even without fire-water.

The miners, mostly tenderfeet, were caught unawares by the early snows on that high mountain region. It was only November, scarcely winter at home. But here it kept snowing, the snow piling up in huge drifts, and it was cold. Also their provisions were getting dangerously low. Somebody had to go to town to stock up, but nobody wanted to leave the diggings. Nobody was willing to give up for even a week the excitement of blasting a new streak of ore from this fabulous mountain. The only way to decide was to cast lots. Buck Rogers lost.

With $500 in dust, he started out, promising to be back in a week. But he ran into one storm after the other, his horse went lame, he lost half a day by taking a wrong trail in a blinding blizzard. It took him a week just to get to town. He staggered up the main street, thankful to be alive. So thankful he had to have a drink to celebrate.

As always with Buck, one drink led to another, and another. One spree lengthened from an hour, to a night, to a week—and it took Buck six weeks to recover, and all the gold dust he had with him was gone.

Fully sober at last, he was tormented by what he had done. Six weeks—and his partners, his pals, back there on Slate Mountain waiting for food! Stealing his share of the gold too, no doubt. In spite of threatened storms and friendly warnings that he would never make it, Buck started out, determined to travel night and day until he reached the men. The nearer he got to Slate Mountain, the worse he felt. A dark presentiment kept growing in his guilty breast, a terrible feeling that he would not find his partners alive. But he kept going, fighting through snow when he was nearly too exhausted to move. Only one more mile—a half mile—a quarter—just around that corner in the gulch—

But where was the camp? Where were the diggings, and the men?

Only an endless white stretch of silent snow, smooth and still as a vast blanket untouched for centuries, met his baffled gaze.

Awestruck and horrified, Buck Rogers turned and slowly made his way back to town. His eyes had a blank look and he only mumbled foolishly when friends tried to find out what was wrong. One night he disappeared from Red Cliff and was never seen again.

A miner, who occupied his room after Buck left, found a notebook with a few remarks about the mine and its location. The miner went by himself to find it. He learned what had stunned poor Buck—a giant snowslide had covered the camp, leaving nothing to show that a short time ago twenty-nine rich and happy miners had lived there. Nothing to show that twenty-nine lives had perished there.

The slide had changed the entire appearance of the country. But the miner was lucky enough to dig where he finally found a tunnel, fragments of tools, human bones and pieces of ore, all tossed and thrown together by the tremendous force of the slide.

The miner covered up what he had found. This rich discovery was going to be his. But he recorded the necessary details for locating his claim (when he could get to the courthouse) and left the papers hidden in his cabin. He guardedly told a little of the story to his closest friend, a man named James Fulford. Two weeks later the old miner was killed in a tavern brawl.

James Fulford lost no time in grief and none in outfitting himself for the trip to Slate Mountain. He searched his friend's cabin and found the papers. Now the gold would be his alone. A month later he was seen wandering up a gulch, looking gaunt and feverish, muttering about getting back to town in a couple days.

The next day a heavy snow began to fall. Fulford did not show up in town, nor was he ever seen again. His body has never been found.

Until today neither has the fabulous gold mine nor its $100,000 pile of ore, buried along with twenty-nine miners, been found. But even a snowslide with all its power does not destroy the gold in the rock. The treasure is still there, and one of these days some lucky searcher may find it.

Also told by Editha L. Watson in the *Daily Sentinel* (Grand Junction), 1936

Lost Mine of Big Baldy

Back in the summer of 1860 when Lafayette Seaman, first coroner of Summit County, was working his placer mine at Lincoln, two burly red-bearded men stopped to watch him. They did not ask any questions —they just watched. As Seaman shovelled dirt into his long tom, the one without any upper teeth opined this was harder work than farming back in Missouri.

"You're right, Hank," drawled the other, who had three upper teeth. "But we'll be making ten thousand a day, 'stead of a few copper cents."

They ambled off, and Seaman smiled to himself. Ten thousand a day! These tenderfeet, rushing to the West, expecting to pick up a fortune in a week, had a surprise coming.

The red-bearded Missourians slept all day. Every night after dark they vanished over the ridge. Before dawn they returned, packing on their backs sacks full of white gouge or clay. Out of every hundred pounds of clay they panned an ounce of gold.

Nobody knew where they worked every night. The miners at Lincoln were curious, but they were all busy with their own work. Besides, the Missourians were huge fellows, and wore long hunting knives and ugly-looking guns in their belts.

Jim Jorgenson, either braver or more curious than the rest, tried to trail them. He claimed they skirted the top of Big Baldy, and was satisfied that any mine with such unusual white clay could easily be located, once the Missourians left.

They did not leave until the streams froze, and all the prospectors moved to Breckenridge for the winter. In 1861, when war broke out, Hank and his partner left for Missouri, and nobody in Colorado ever saw them again.

Jorgenson led a searching party to Big Baldy. They found no mine with white clay. Other parties took up the search, but to this day the secret of the white-clay mine with its rich gold deposit remains with the two burly red-bearded Missourians who would be long in their graves by now.

Also told by George Jarvis Bancroft in the *Rocky Mountain News*, 1914

11

Lost Mine of Lost Man Gulch

Often, as the snowslides which have covered the landscape throughout the freezing winters in the high mountains melt with spring, tragic discoveries are made. Frank Brown (one of the men who later attempted to navigate the Colorado Canyon and lost his life in Desolation Canyon) learned this one day in the spring of 1880. At the time Brown was the manager of the Farwell properties at Farwell (an early name for Independence). He was making his way on what is now the main highway from Leadville to Aspen, not far from the then-wealthy camp of Independence.

As he looked about for a place to spend the night in the shelter of a ledge, he noticed a dark object. Thinking it was a dead animal, he investigated, and found to his horror it was the frozen body of a man. From the attire and the pack nearby with mining tools, it appeared that the man had been a prospector. The unfortunate miner, probably on his way back to his mine, had been caught by a snowslide which had hidden him from view until the spring thaw.

Miners from Independence examined the body and remembered having seen the man the summer before, prospecting at the head of Lost Man Gulch, a branch of the Roaring Fork.

It was also remembered that in the fall of 1879 this man appeared in Leadville with a pack of extremely rich ore. The ore was bought at a princely sum by Berdell and Witherell. The miner, despite the curiosity his gold aroused, refused to say where he had obtained it or where he was from. He was seen only a few times after that. Then he disappeared, until Brown discovered the frozen body on the mountainside.

There is no proof that the rich ore came from this locality, but the chances are that it did. Gold ore was later mined up Lincoln Gulch in the direction of the town of Ruby, south of where the man's body was found. But exactly where his mine was is still a secret—for gold ore that rich has yet to be re-discovered in the mountains at the head of Lost Man Gulch.

Also told by George Jarvis Bancroft in the *Rocky Mountain News*, 1914

Into Thin Air

In January, 1859, George A. Jackson trudged up Clear Creek by himself and panned enough gold at the present site of Idaho Springs to make the first important placer-gold discovery in Colorado.

He was also the man who hid $10,000 worth of gold dust in buckskin bags that have never been found—even though the location is no secret, but definitely known.

The lost gold is not what he found in Clear Creek in January, 1859. He made another rich find high on the top of the range in Middle Park twelve years later. After Jackson made his first discoveries, he returned to serve in the Civil War and to farm in Missouri for several years. Then he and a friend returned to Colorado to go prospecting, and they made a strike.

Realizing the strike was rich and fearing unfriendly Indians, the two men returned to Georgetown. They wanted to get together a dozen men or so to further explore the new area, which was four or five miles from Rabbit Ears Peak. They had no trouble finding ten prospectors willing to go to Middle Park for gold. As soon as they reached the spot, they got to work building a camp, with cabin and corral.

Jackson, at the end of a hard day, relaxed by carving his name on a tree at the corner of the cabin.

In a short time, more than $10,000 in gold was panned from the stream. The miners stored their wealth in buckskin bags and hid them under the earth in a corner of the cabin.

This was when a band of blood-thirsty Indian warriors descended on the peaceful little camp, high on a mountainside. The prospectors managed to hide and later made their way through the mountains and over Berthoud Pass to Georgetown. All but Jackson decided the West was far too wild for them, and returned to their Eastern homes.

By now the heavy snows had started, and it was impossible for Jackson to go back for the gold. He told a close friend where the mine and the hidden gold were, and they made plans to go there the instant weather permitted in the spring.

Before spring came, Jackson was recalled to Missouri on serious family business with the agreement that the friend would forward his share.

His friend and another miner made the journey into the wild country that June. On Walton Creek, near where the old Steamboat road crossed, they found the cabin and corral. They found the tree with Jackson's name on it. There could be no mistake—this was the place.

Eagerly they went to work in the cabin, digging up the old dirt floor, covered with debris. They turned the earth upside down from wall to wall. There were no buckskin bags filled with precious dust.

Jackson, they decided, may have been mixed-up in his directions. So they kept on digging, not stopping until they had explored to a good depth all around the cabin, the corral and under the tree with Jackson's name on it.

There was no gold.

Who had been in the deserted, lonely place since the Indians? Because of the heavy snows, it was unlikely that any white man had been there.

Maybe—and this is the more generally accepted theory—Jackson and his miners, wily and shrewd where their gold was concerned, really hid the gold farther away, perhaps in some secret cave nearby. If so, it still awaits the lucky finder in that remote, sky-high wilderness.

Also told by Editha L. Watson in the *Dolores Star*, 1935

The Reynolds' Bandit Treasure

Of all the hidden treasure legends in Colorado, none is more famous than the story of the Jim Reynolds gang's gold, buried in the wild high country of upper Deer Creek, above the town of Shaffers Crossing. That it was buried there—the loot of stagecoach robberies, perhaps amounting to $75,000 in gold, $100,000 in currency and diamonds and other jewelry—there is no reason to doubt. Too many signs, as told by the robbers themselves, have been found by hordes of searchers in the nearly hundred years that have passed since the treasure was buried.

The Reynolds gang was a group of twenty-two guerrilla desperadoes who came north from Texas in the early 1860's, eager to take advantage of the vast wealth pouring from the Shining Mountains of Colorado. They did not intend to spend time and work prospecting or digging. They had an easier, quicker way to get rich—robbing stagecoaches.

By 1864 distrust and fighting among themselves reduced the gang to a small band of Jim and John Reynolds and seven others. Then they robbed the Fairplay-Denver coach close to Kenosha Pass. They got $40,000 in currency (which was wrapped in silk oil cloth) and three cans of gold dust valued at $23,000. Moving eastward along the Platte, they continued to rob everyone they met. Then they learned an enraged posse was hot on their trail—a group of Summit County miners, organized by Gen. David Cook, chief of government detectives in Colorado.

Racing for cover, the bandits made camp on Deer Creek, west of Shaffers Crossing. As the posse came closer and closer, the two Reynolds brothers, leaders of the gang, parted from the rest to hide the stolen loot near the head of Deer and Elk Creeks on the side of Mt. Logan.

A short time later, the posse crept up on them and opened fire. One bandit was killed instantly, but the others fled through the underbrush. Not far from Canon City, a detachment of the First Colorado Cavalry captured the horseless outlaws, with the exception of one named Jack Stowe, and John Reynolds, who escaped across the Arkansas River.

The prisoners were brought to Denver, tried by a military commission for highway robbery and ordered to Fort Leavenworth for punishment. On the third morning of the trip to the fort, the men were taken from the coach, manacled together, blindfolded and shot to death. Jim Reynolds grimly refused to make any statement about the buried gold before he was shot.

John Reynolds and Stowe, the only remaining members of the notorious gang, were next heard of in Santa Fe, where Stowe was killed in a gun fight. Reynolds lived for some time in Santa Fe; then

A STAGECOACH WAS ROBBED ON KENOSHA PASS

with a pal named Albert Brown headed for Denver in 1871. On the way they raided a Mexican ranch. Reynolds was mortally wounded, but before he died he told Brown about the treasure hidden at the head of Deer Creek, giving these directions:

"Go above Geneva Gulch a little ways and you'll find where one of our horses mired down and we had to leave it there. At the head of the gulch, you turn to the right and follow a mountain around a little farther. And just above the head of Deer Creek, you'll find an old prospector's shaft running back into the mountain at about timberline. It's back there in the hole, pard. We walled the hole up with stones and stuck a butcher knife into a tree about four feet from the ground, broke the handle off and left it pointing to the mouth of the hole."

Brown went to Geneva Gulch, only to find a forest fire had destroyed the timber, and he was unable to locate a trace of the treasure. But he did find the skeleton of a horse that was mired and left to die.

According to another story, one of the prisoners before he died by the guard's gunfire, said the loot was buried three or four miles from the main Reynolds camp, and was marked by a crude dagger made from a file, driven into a dead tree a few hundred feet from where the gold was buried. Jim Reynolds drove the dagger into the tree part way, pulled it out, broke off the point, then drove the point deep into the tree ahead of the rest of the blade. If anybody ever pulled the broken blade out of the tree, the point would still be left.

In the early 1900's an elderly man by the name of Tex Taylor came to the Platte Valley. He claimed his uncle was a member of the notorious Reynolds gang, had escaped the posse and gone to California to live. Before he died, this uncle gave Tex a map of the buried treasure —the reason Tex had come to Colorado. The map stated that up a certain creek there was a stone barricade behind which several men

15

could lie and guard the steep trail to a little hidden park where the main camp was. Beyond the camp was a corral. One of the gang, Tex's uncle said, was shot in a fight and buried a mile and a half above the camp under a big spruce tree. A dagger was carved on this tree to mark the grave.

Tex died after many fruitless searches. Maybe the most important part of the directions died with him for he never told how far, nor in what direction from the tree with the broken dagger, the treasure was buried.

Vernon Crow, who in 1933 had located some mining claims on Handcart Creek only a few miles from the gang's major camp area, was reminded of the old story (which had happened more than seventy years before) when he saw, sticking out of an old long-dead timberline tree, a knife-handle, dark with rust. Working the handle, he brought out a crude dagger made from a file—with the point missing. He searched a little, but being busy with his own mines, gave up treasure-hunting.

He did save the old dagger. Every time he saw it, it worried him—was there really a great fortune hidden nearby? Maybe he was stupid not to try to find it. But it was 1938 before he got to it, and then he found the hidden park with the old stone breastworks, and above the park the ruins of an old stockade corral. Almost a year later, he noticed a funny-looking mark on a large dead spruce across the creek—a crude cross carved into the trunk. A few feet from the tree was a rock like a gravestone, set in the ground. Crow dug and found the skeleton of a man, buried with his boots on. But here his search bogged down, and we have no record of his trying again.

The trail up Handcart Gulch starts at the ghost town of Hall Valley, ten miles northwest of Grant. It is a steep climb, and the trail very faint, on up through aspen and spruce for half a mile to the stone breastworks. Uptrail is the little hidden park in an aspen grove. Still higher, it levels out into a big square area, and to the right the bank drops steeply to Handcart Creek. Around this corral area runs a deep trench, where once a solid wall of logs stood upright. Many of the logs, with axe marks visible, still lie where they fell.

A mile upstream is the grave of the bandit that Crow discovered. Near the grave is a spring of water rusty with iron—and that iron is one reason the Reynolds gold has not been found, for electronic detectors cannot be used in an area heavy with iron. A magnetic compass spins wildly.

That the gold was actually buried not far from the tree with the broken dagger is certain. But around the tree are endless places to dig. Still, every spring optimistic treasure-hunters head for the region reached by Deer, Elk and Handcart Creeks, faith burning and hopes soaring. Somebody is going to be lucky and dig in the right spot.

After all, the chance of finding a hundred thousand or so in greenbacks and in gold dust is worth some backache, and months—even years—of searching.

Also told by D. J. Cook in *Hands Up*, 1897; the *Denver Post*, 1947; *Rocky Mountain News*, 1949.

(See Frontispiece Map for Location)

Cache la Poudre Lost Mine

Hans the Dutchman and Mike the Irishman were bosom buddies who came in 1860 to the military fort of Fort Collins, then the middle of a wilderness that was Kansas Territory. Loaded with gold, they stayed at the fort just long enough for a good spree, then vanished across the wide gray prairie in the direction of the Shining Mountains, shadowy purple against the western sky.

Had this happened but once, the soldiers at the fort would have paid little attention. But it happened time and again. Always the two buddies arrived loaded with gold, had themselves a spree, sobered up and disapeared. No matter how drunk they were, they never revealed where they came from, nor where they went. The curious soldiers, awed by all the gold, tried their best to find out.

Finally they hired a celebrated Indian scout to follow Hans and Mike. He kept them in sight for three days, and then took off after a deer, sure he could pick up the trail again in a few hours. But a snowstorm covered the trail, and all the Indian scout could report was that the two men went straight up the Cache la Poudre.

The next time the Dutchman and Irishman came back, they bought a donkey so they could pack in bigger supplies and pack out more gold. Soon the load was too heavy for the donkey, so they traded it for an ox. Even the ox was over-burdened with the heavy load of gold ore the two miners brought in.

Then, to the soldiers' surprise, the prospectors came tramping wearily on foot, carrying their gold on their backs and mourning their ox, who had been killed by a bear right outside their cabin door. That time they drank more than usual, began to quarrel, and suddenly the Irishman landed a blow on Hans' head that killed him.

Now, the soldiers exulted, they would find out about that mine. They seized Mike and told him they would hang him unless he told them where his mine was.

Mike glared defiantly, bearded jaws locked tight. Even when the soldiers put a rope around his neck and led him to a cottonwood tree, he only gritted his teeth harder and glared more fiercely. The soldiers, planning only to give him a good scare, threw the rope over a limb and pulled him up in the air for half a minute.

When they let him down, he was dead. What with the long trek from the hills, the drunken spree and the fight with his buddy, Mike needed only a bit of strangulation to stop his heart.

With both men dead, the mysterious mine was no doubt lost forever.

But prospectors kept looking, without finding a trace of cabin or mine, until Billy Meline in 1899 came to Fort Collins from Nebraska and got a job in a sawmill. He often visited Manhattan, a small mining camp thirty miles west. Here he heard talk about the lost mine of Mike and Hans. He could not rest for dreaming about it. He was going to find that mine and be the richest man in Nebraska.

Just about this time, a little boy was lost in the mountains, and everybody in town went to look for him, searching all night. In the morning, the boy rode back by himself, surprised at all the commotion he had caused—he had spent a good night at a cabin up in a gulch. He had built a fire in the fireplace, found some canned beans to eat— and best of all, he had found rocks with pretty gold specks lying on the rickety plank table. He brought back with him some bleached bones— bear bones, he hoped. He found them just outside the cabin door.

Billy Meline was almost out of his mind with excitement—it was clear the boy had stumbled on the lost camp of Hans and Mike! Nobody in town was interested; they had more serious work to do than look for needles in a haystack.

Billy was all set to venture forth himself when Amos, eighty-year-old prospector, offered to go along. A friend warned Billy that the old man got crazy spells. He had been in a fight with a bear some years ago. Ever since at any excitement or at the sight of a wild animal, he went berserk. But Billy felt he could handle the old man, and so they started out.

They had no trouble finding the cabin the boy had discovered. A faint trail led from the cabin, and suddenly there was the black mouth of a tunnel in the side of the mountain. The old man yelled with excitement and rushed in, without even waiting to light his candle. He came rushing out just as fast—and after him a big brown bear and her two cubs.

The old prospector went berserk. Even though the bear ambled off into the underbrush with her cubs, Amos grabbed his gun from his belt and pointed it at Billy.

"I've got to kill you—leave something for them to eat while I get away!" he shouted, and even as his shaking withered finger reached for the trigger, Billy lunged and caught the oldster about the knees. The bullet went into the air harmlessly, the shot echoing and re-echoing through the quiet mountain forest.

It took all Billy's strength to get the wild old man back to town. In doing it he sprained his ankle, which made it impossible to go back to the lost mine for several weeks. But he wasn't worried—he remembered where it was: on the north slope of Black Mountain, near the top, in heavy timber. It would not be hard to locate again.

18

He looked and looked—for years. He never found it. He got to believing it had all been a dream, a crazy dream with a crazy old man prospector, and the cabin only a ghost cabin. Sometimes he thought he heard Hans and Dutchman and Mike the Irishman chuckling in their shadowy beards.

Just another lost Colorado gold mine. This one has the white bones of an ox before a cabin door to mark it from the others.

Also told by George Jarvis Bancroft in the *Rocky Mountain News*, 1914

Hicks Mountain

Douglas McLean had been restored to health in the clear, life-giving air of Colorado. After two years in bed with tuberculosis, it was a blessing for him to be able to take a walk through the pine and aspen woods after his day's work on an Evergreen ranch. As the warm summer days of 1895 merged into the sunny brisk days of autumn, he found he could take longer walks. He could even do a little rabbit hunting—always noticing rock formations, for nobody lived in the Colorado mountains without getting something of the prospector's fever. Gold could be anywhere—it was everywhere.

As an Eastern tenderfoot who had come West for his health, he knew very little about veins and ores—yet he discovered a vein running a thousand dollars in gold to the ton!

The vein has been lost from that day to this.

He had wandered a little too far into the dense timber of Mt. Bergen, then called Mt. Strain, on the side closest to Hicks Mountain. He became hopelessly lost from ten in the morning until five at night. Finding himself in a small gulch after hours of wandering, he was hurrying a little desperately, as it had begun to snow. In the thin air of the Rockies, it is impossible to hurry without stopping every so often for breath. McLean, in spite of his anxiety, stopped to draw air into empty lungs, leaning against a ledge under a high earthen bank. Suddenly his pulses leaped—what beautiful pink and white quartz! The vein was at least eighteen inches wide. He broke off pieces of the out-cropping. In the poor light of dusk, and with the prospects of a freezing night spent in the open alarming him, he did not pay too much attention to the locality.

He stuffed the ore specimens in his pocket and plunged on, fighting the fast-increasing snow. Luckily the gulch came out at a small creek, which he followed, and reached the Witter ranch. He was so grateful to be safe and out of the storm, that he forgot about his specimens until the next day. Then he studied them with unbelieving eyes—for he held in his shaking hands rose quartz, chockful of coarse gold!

The storm that had started the day before grew worse, but McLean could not wait to get to Denver to report his find. Next day he took the

HICKS MOUNTAIN IS AT RIGHT OF RANCH

stage to the city, where he showed the specimens to his doctor, F. J.
Bancroft. Dr. Bancroft provided him with a pony and blank location
notices, and McLean hurried back to look for the rich ledge. In the
deep snow that had piled up in the gulch, he could not even find the
outlines of his ledge.

One storm after the other, in the way of the Continental Divide
country, followed the first one, and McLean was forced to abandon his
search until spring. The next two summers—1896 and 1897—he
tramped every inch of the south slope of Hicks Mountain without finding the slightest trace of his ledge or the rose quartz outcropping.

He always insisted that the ledge was in either a branch of Witter
Gulch or in the next one coming into Bear Creek below Witter, and
that it was at the bottom of the gulch under a high earthen bank. It is
possible that the bank caved in under spring thaws, covering the ledge
and changing the entire contours of the gulch. It is also possible that
as a tenderfoot worried about spending a freezing night in the open—
in his case, so lately an invalid, likely fatal—he was completely confused. He may have wandered farther around Hicks Mountain than
he thought.

Whatever the reason, the vein has never again been found, nor
has any quartz of that description been reported from the district.
McLean gave up the search and returned East about 1910. But prospectors in that part of the hills still keep their eyes open for an outcropping of rose quartz, studded with coarse gold, assaying at least one
thousand dollars to the ton.

Also told by George Jarvis Bancroft in the *Rocky Mountain News*, 1914

Lost Mine of Stevens Gulch

Henry Jackson, an old Negro, lived near the mouth of Stevens Gulch, the first big gulch this side of Strontia Springs, a station on the Platte Canyon branch of the Colorado and Southern Railway. In the early 1900's, Henry, gnarled and grizzled and gray, did not even know how old he was. His mother was a half-breed squaw, and he had lived with the Indians long before the white men came to Colorado.

When he was a little boy, he declared, the Indians used to go up Stevens Gulch and bring down ore in buckskin bags. Then the squaws would crush it up in crude mattes and wash it in a trough made of a hollowed-out log. When the sand was washed away, they would gather up the gold and put it in quills of eagle and wild goose feathers. Later on they would take it back to the "River" (Missouri River) and trade it to the white men for beads, whiskey and ammunition.

As Henry's story went, some time after the Civil War, two young men stopped by his cabin one evening. They were from St. Joseph, Missouri; listened in astonishment to Henry's account of the Indians' mine and of the years there had been a steady flow of gold from it. The old Negro had not been interested enough to go up the gulch to see this piece of mountain that must be nearly solid with the precious metal. But the two young men lost no time in exploring Stevens Gulch.

They had little trouble locating the mine. They had more trouble getting an ox wagon up the narrow, rugged gulch in order to move their ore to market. It took them months, but finally they had a wagonload of rich ore. They took it to St. Joseph, and sold it. While there, they made a crude map showing the location of their find and the hiding-place of their tools.

They started back to their mine in 1867. They evidently had a road or trail somewhere near the present Jarre Canyon road, for their murdered bodies and the ox wagon were found near Devil's Head mountain. It was supposed the Indians had killed them.

Later on one of the relatives of the two young men sent a copy of the crude map to Henry Jackson and asked him to try to find the mine. He searched diligently, but was unsuccessful.

Yet, in 1910 he found the rusted remains of some very old-fashioned mining tools. They were concealed in a clump of dense underbrush, and the location agreed with the point shown on the map.

Strange to say, a young man named Carl R. Johnson brought indirect substantiation of this story. In 1911 he was hunting rabbits around the head of Stevens Gulch. Johnson noticed several veins of rusty quartz and picked up a piece or two from each vein. Altogether he brought home quite a pocketful of rock.

Later on he was working in a testing plant in Denver, and as the machinery was handy, he crushed up the whole pocketful together and panned the lot. What was his surprise to get a good string of colors!

It was not likely that all of the quartz carried gold. It was more likely that one piece was rich and the rest worthless. So in 1912 he went back and hunted the same ground over, but he found only barren quartz. There was one place, however, which he could never find again. He remembered that he had pushed into the bushes because he thought he saw a rabbit go in them and had discovered a little tunnel.

Johnson remembered picking up a piece of good-looking quartz at this clump of bushes. It is possible that this was the rich piece that yielded the colors and that the little hole or tunnel was the lost Indians' mine. If so, the mine is still there.

Also told by George Jarvis Bancroft in the *Rocky Mountain News*, 1914

Devil's Head Stands Guard

Over nine-thousand feet high against the western sky, a landmark clearly visible for seventy-five miles, rears the jagged, sinister figure of Devil's Head Mountain. It looks down arrogantly on its wild gulches and thick timber, almost impassable, and many are the weird stories of outlaws, ghosts and death told about this evil-looking peak. Lost treasure stories too—and one of the most famous concerns the robbery of a government train in the 1870's by a gang who got away with $60,000 in gold eagles.

Devil's Head made an ideal hideout for outlaws in the early days. Even today, desperadoes will seek cover on its rugged slopes, but with a national forest fire-lookout atop the Head, it is not as safe a hideout as it was back in the '70's.

The bandits who had robbed the government train hid in the forest near Devil's Head. The posse pursuing them consisted of men who had lived in that area and knew it well. As the posse drew closer and closer to the outlaws, they hurriedly buried their loot of $60,000, stuck a long knife into a towering spruce at the head of the treasure grave, and got out of the country.

Little is known of the outlaws from then on. Something must have kept them from returning to get their stolen gold. Or they may have tried many times and were unable in that fierce, untracked wilderness to find the tree—so like ten thousand others—with a knife stuck in it.

In 1923, fifty years after the robbery, an old man, grizzled and bent, was seen day after day wandering on the mountain. A forester at the lookout station kept watching him. What was he looking for, and why was he fumblingly trying to cover up his tracks? He was far too old and rheumatic to be climbing the rugged ascents for the fun of it.

Finally the forester trailed and stopped him. The old man lifted furtive, alarmed eyes, claiming he was doing no harm—he was just looking.

"Looking for what?" the forester prodded gently. There was something pathetic and broken about the scared old man, his shifting eyes and shaking hands. For a time he would not say anything. But at last he told the forester he had been a member of the gang so many years ago that robbed the government train and hid the gold—under a tree with a knife stuck in it.

"I know it was right about here," the old man insisted. "I never forgot just where we was—I knew some day I'd be back. But now—" He looked about him blankly at the open area where blackened stumps of trees were all that remained of the deep forest.

"These woods burned—big forest fire—years ago," the forester said. "Your tree with the knife in it went up in smoke."

The old man's watery eyes scanned the barren miles of mountain slope. "Take a heap of digging to find the spot now," he quavered. "Guess I ain't got that many years left—to dig up all this."

So far nobody else has tried to dig up that mountain slope either. Searchers have looked from time to time, arguing that the bandits were in a hurry with the posse on their backs and could not have dug too deep a hole. Yet no buried treasure has come to light.

With the erosion of weather forever eating away at the earth, maybe the edge of an iron-banded box sticking out of the ground will be seen soon—by someone willing to look hard, inch by inch, on the mighty slope of Devil's Head's charred shoulder.

Also told by Editha L. Watson in the *Daily Sentinel* (Grand Junction), 1936

Illusive Topaz Jewels

Somewhere on the steep dark slopes of Devil's Head is a lost topaz mine.

The topaz is a beautiful gem, ranging in color from the golden shade usually associated with it to ruby, brownish (or smoky), milky blue and colorless. Some of those idly picked up in various places on Devil's Head are the finest yet discovered in the United States. But the mother lode, the rich deposit from which these single specimens have been washed down, has remained lost since its original discovery by W. B. Smith in 1883. He accidentally came on the jewels while prospecting for other minerals on the mountain.

Dr. A. J. Argall, member of a prominent family associated with Leadville mining, was an ardent gem and rock hound. He became interested in the Devil's Head deposit when he read an old article by R. T. Cross telling of Smith's discovery. According to Smith, the pocket in which he found the unusually excellent topaz gems was of irregular shape about fifty feet long, from two to fifteen wide and averaging four in depth. Owing to the disintegration of the rock at the surface, many crystals had been carried quite a distance down the mountainside and were badly worn and broken.

23

DEVIL'S HEAD SPARKLED WITH TOPAZ JEWELS

Later in 1885, the topaz deposit was completely documented in Geological Survey Professional Paper No. 20, by W. B. Smith himself. He did not give the exact location but, as he remembered it, the vein was on the southwest side of a creek. Smith also said that a note telling of his discovery had been published in the American Journal of Science for December, 1883, by Rev. R. T. Cross of Denver.

Dr. Argall and his wife spent the summer of 1935 looking for the mine. They did find three fine gems—orphan stones, separated from the parent mine by miles possibly. These three stones only made them more anxious to discover the source, somewhere on the west side of the mountain. But they could never find it.

Massive old Devil's Head is chuckling in his beard of thick black spruce and pine over the many gem collectors through the past eighty years who have picked up some of the finest specimens of golden, ruby, smoky, and clear topaz ever found in this country, but can't locate the mine itself.

Devil's Head has many secrets in its impenetrable forests, its rocky gulches and mysterious caves, and the topaz mine remains one of them.

Also told by Dr. A. J. Argall in conversation, 1936

SECTION 4-A

(See Frontispiece Map for Location)

The Third Gravestone

The tremendous fortunes found in the West from 1849 on lured every kind of man on a frantic chase of the golden phantom. The majority were willing to work for their gold—search out a good claim and mine it by hard digging, timbering, dynamiting. But there were always those who tried to get it the easy way: stealing.

In Sacramento, California, in '49, a band of eight men worked together, the easy way. In the next twelve years they accumulated $100,000 in gold, a neat fortune even if it must be divided eight ways. Everything had gone well, but in 1862 they understood that the law was on their trail, and they set out across the Rockies with their loot.

They reached what is now the town of Clifford, Colorado, in safety, and made a pretty far-fetched resolution to live quietly and lawfully from then on. But they heard of a stagecoach coming through carrying an army payroll. Just one more robbery would not hurt. An army payroll would add considerably to their $100,000. They made their expert plans (which had always worked without a slip) and were ready for the stagecoach as it came thundering out of the East with the paymaster, a few soldiers—and the payroll.

The soldiers, it seemed, were also ready, sending the amazed and outraged bandits fleeing for their lives. The soldiers followed and killed six.

The two surviving were elated that there were only two instead of eight to share the hundred thousand. Yet they still had a big problem—escaping with such a heavy burden, and getting their gold safely back East. After much arguing back and forth, they agreed it was best to bury it, mark it carefully, and come back for it later—when the soldiers had forgotten all about them.

They made three mounds, shaped like graves. At the head of each they chiselled their names on a flat stone like a grave marker with a false date—1857. They put "Unknown" and the same date on the third. The mounds made a triangle, and in the center of the triangle they buried the gold. It would be there when they got back.

They headed East, and for many years nothing is known of either. It was more than twenty years later, in the '80's, that a stranger appeared in the area around Clifford. He was a small, tight-lipped, furtive-eyed man, talking little, and obviously searching for something. He went out on long, lonely treks by himself.

The one person he did talk to was a sheepherder. The stranger explained that he was looking for a treasure he had buried in '62. After several weeks of searching, the stranger returned East. But before leaving, he told the sheepherder about the three gravestones with the date 1857. Those rocks were somewhere around, the stranger said, and inside the triangle they formed, safe in the earth, lay a hundred thousand in gold.

The herder told his boss, James Will, owner of the ranch, who organized searching parties that tramped the ground almost inch by inch. No flat rocks, grave markers with rudely chiseled inscriptions, were ever found.

The legend of the false tombstones faded with the passing years. Half a century later, in 1931, a man named Elkins discovered one of the stones, overgrown with shrubbery. Now the old story came to full life again, and a flock of people rushed to the area, every one certain he could dig up a fortune in gold. Not only were the other two false gravestones never found, but no treasure of any sort. Disappointed dreamers departed, returning to the humdrum grind of daily toil.

In November of 1934 excitement flared again when a second stone was found by T. C. Hatton of Clifford. The flat rock bore the inscription: "D. Grover and Joseph Foxe Lawe—Aug. 8, 1857."

Treasure-seekers again swarmed over Will's sheep ranch, hoping to locate the third stone. As no gold had been uncovered near the two already found, the treasure must surely be buried under the third one.

The search went on and on. The third gravestone has never been found, nor has a fortune in gold coins.

It is possible that the stranger who came back in the '80's actually found it, but did not tell. It is also possible that his partner in crime had come back before him, removed it and told no one, certainly not a partner who would demand his rightful $50,000. Why should he talk, when just by keeping still he could have the whole fortune for himself?

But it is also possible—and the people of Clifford believe this— that the gold is still there. Where is the third grave marker? When that is found, and no treasure buried near it, then the people of Clifford may be ready to admit the gold has already been removed.

Until then—many are still searching for the third and last mock gravestone. And nearby, safe in its earthen grave, is the glittering pile of a hundred thousand in gold.

Also told by Editha L. Watson in the *Aspen Times,* 1935

SECTION 1 - B

(See Frontispiece Map for Location)

Pillars of Gold

Two towering pillars of stone stand silent lonely guard to a small valley, running into Colorado from the wild and precipitous mountains of northern New Mexico west of the Rio Grande River. Back in the 1800's when the Spanish conquerors were roaming the great West, some of the padres and soldiers stopped to examine the august and mighty monuments.

The pillars were made of gold!

Not entirely, of course. But most of the stones were pieces of rich gold ore which had, no doubt, been found not too far away.

In that pleasant little valley, distinguished from hundreds of others only by the bleak, majestic pillars, the padres and soldiers became miners until they had dug all the gold they could possibly carry with them.

Others, in the years that followed, saw the pillars, but considered them only a freakish geologic formation and passed them by.

Except Mike O'Leary, who arrived a century after the Spanish had been there. The rumors are that he stumbled on some ancient workings on one of his prospecting trips. At least, he appeared in Parrott City on the La Plata River, southwest of Durango, with enough gold to pay for a spree lasting several weeks. No matter how drunk he was, he clammed up when asked where he had found the gold.

When he sobered up, he disappeared—only to show up in Animas City on the Animas River south of Silverton, several months later with another small fortune in gold.

Other prospectors tried to follow O'Leary when he headed back into the wild country. But O'Leary was as wily and clever as any of the prospectors of that time. He trusted nobody, searched in solitude, and enjoyed keeping a secret. Discovery of a rich strike meant not only hordes of miners hot on the trail of gold, but claim-jumpers and desperadoes ready to use guns and knives to get what they wanted.

So nobody ever caught up with O'Leary. He slipped out of sight when his gold was gone; he slipped into town with plenty more a few months, or maybe a year, later. All that was known was that he hid out somewhere in the valley of the Stone Pillars.

Finally someone remarked that O'Leary had not been around for a long time. Parrott City began watching for him, but he never came.

He might have traveled on to California. He might have found his grave beside the faithful mine that had paid him well.

But where was the mine? Was it the same one that had poured out riches for the Spanish padres? Or are there two fabulous mines in the valley of the Stone Pillars?

Either, or both, are no doubt still rich, waiting for a new discoverer. Neither the padres nor Mike O'Leary, with their crude tools, could have exhausted the mines whose gold built the Stone Pillars.

Also told by Editha Watson in the *Herald Democrat* (Leadville), 1935

Navaho Curse

Anything back as far as 1849 is considered ancient history in the West. But the legends of buried treasure defy all rules and break all laws. The tale of a fabulous Navaho gold and silver mine starts years before that—in the year 1776. According to the story, the Spanish exploration party of Dominguez and Escalante, roaming through the area now known as the Four Corners, where New Mexico, Arizona, Colorado and Utah meet, discovered a placer. Reports of its richness filtered down through the decades but not of the placer's exact location, which was obscure. The tale acquired additions which spoke of a silver mine on the hill above.

Finally almost a century after the first Spanish report, two cavalrymen, Merrick and Mitchell, were high on a butte and discovered a rude forge along with some silver and gold nuggets. The butte was south of Cortez in southwestern Colorado, close to the Four Corners. The Navahos warned the soldiers to keep out. But Merrick and Mitchell stole back at night, found the mine near by, and took out ore samples which assayed $800 to the ton. In 1879 Jim Jarvis of Cortez financed a company to develop the soldiers' mine with Merrick and Mitchell retaining half-interest. In their eagerness and excitement, Merrick and Mitchell sneaked back to the mine for more samples.

When they did not return, a searching party was sent out. The two bodies, riddled with arrows, and a fresh supply of ore that they were carrying were found in a gulch bottom. The mine itself could not be found. The posse that found the bodies believed that the angry Navahos buried the mine entrance.

Many years after the death of Merrick and Mitchell, a priest appeared in Prescott, Arizona, with a strange story which had been told him by a dying man in a Denver hospital. Ths man said he and two others had taken $75,000 in gold from a placer mine on the Navaho reservation in the Four Corners district. But they had had to flee for their lives when the Indians discovered their presence. They had traveled south through western New Mexico, crossed the Mogollon mountains, followed the Gila river to the Verde, and finally reached Prescott.

On the way his two companions died, leaving him with the gold.

He was certain that the Indians—or the Great Spirit—were following him, and that as long as he carried the gold, he was in danger of death. So he buried his fortune under a boulder shaped like a man kneeling. The rock was near a spring at the foot of a mountain past which a stream flowed into a small valley, near Prescott. In a tree a few paces away, he cut a small cross above a half circle. He himself wanted nothing more to do with the gold, cursed by the Navahos. But he begged the priest to recover it for the use of the hospital. This would remove the curse.

The priest found the signs—a boulder that did look something like a praying man, and the crude carvings in a tree—but he could not find the chest with its gold treasure.

Was the dying man's gold from the rich Navaho mine?

Whether it was or not, the $75,000 buried near Prescott has never been found.

In 1915, James O'Rourke, a Western congressman, decided to organize a searching party and see what could be found. In one of the canyons in that weird, wild region, O'Rourke discovered a pile of stones over-laying two hundred pounds of silver matte—raw silver roasted in crude furnaces—and also a number of fine gold nuggets.

The searchers' delight was cut short by the arrival of a band of Navahos who resented white people trespassing on their land. The O'Rourke party fled for their lives into a box canyon where the Navaho curses and imprecations echoed after them. They were later rescued by a group of prospectors. The treasure hunters, although they retrieved only a handful of gold nuggets, decided to leave the mine to the Navahos.

A treasure hunter could call himself fortunate if he discovered either the Navahos' mine in Four Corners, Colorado—or the other treasure in its chest, somewhere near the boulder of a praying man, outside Prescott.

Also told by Editha Watson in the *Flagler* (Colorado) *News*, 1935; Richard E. Klinck in *Land of Room Enough and Time Enough*, 1953.

Treasure Mountain

Of all the hidden treasure in Colorado, none, it is claimed, is richer than the millions buried over one hundred and fifty years ago near the top of Wolf Creek Pass some three or four miles south in the direction of Summitville. For eager searchers of many years past, hopes flare and then die—almost. But not quite. As far as is known, the vast horde of gold is still on Treasure Mountain (which is almost on the line between Mineral and Rio Grande Counties). It is reasonable to assume that someone, someday, will find it.

About 1790 a French expedition came to America to investigate the mineral resources of Louisiana Territory. The expedition of three hundred men was composed of skilled miners, mechanics, geologists and soldiers. They made a permanent camp three or four miles from the top of Wolf Creek Pass near Treasure Mountain. At that time, this part of Colorado was unknown to white men except for Spanish exploring parties and trappers. Aside from a few Spanish settlements in northern New Mexico only Indians occupied the land, a veritable paradise for hunters. The Frenchmen not only enjoyed the plentiful game, but did a lot of prospecting and mining. During the summer they took out in gold amounts which vary, according to ancient records, from five million to thirty-three.

Until they were ready to leave, the gold had to be hidden. They made maps telling the locations of the caches, also erected cairns of stones at certain points, and blazed trees with peculiar signs.

Suddenly their paradise of game and gold was exploded by a series of misfortunes. Disease took many; supplies ran low; and the Indians, friendly until now, attacked. Only seventeen got out of the mountains alive. They were forced to resort to cannibalism and cast lots to determine who must die that the rest might live.

Traveling down the Arkansas in boats, the little band was again attacked by Indians, and only five escaped. Of these, three died of hardship, which left only Lebreau, the journalist of the party, and a half-crazed companion. The two men suffered unbelievable privations and narrow escapes from death, but finally reached an Indian village used as a little trading post on the Missouri River. Here Lebreau's companion died, leaving only Lebreau of the three hundred who had left France to return to his homeland.

Through all the dangers and hardships, he had kept a packet of oiled silk untouched. The packet contained the maps and notations of the treasure, and he delivered it safely to his government. A copy was also given his family.

France was having military and economic troubles at home, and the reports of gold half-a-world away were put away and forgotten. After a time they were resurrected and given to a man by the name of LeBlanc, who came to America in 1844 with a party of fifty to look for the gold. This expedition, according to the late Don Archuleta, land and cattle owner of Archuleta County, was guided to Treasure Mountain by Bernardo Sanchez, an elderly Taos Mexican.

Sanchez claimed the Frenchmen worked over the mountain for three years, during which time he packed in supplies from Taos. He swore that no gold, nor anything else, was ever sent out. To move the vast treasure would take at least six hundred mules, and such a cavalcade would have been noticed and remembered by many people.

This group, like the one before it, was attacked by Indians and wiped out. Only Sanchez escaped and made his way to Taos. One of the Frenchmen had given him a clue which both Don Archuleta and Sanchez searched for. There was a certain grave-like mound on which

BURIED TREASURE ABOUNDS IN THE SAN JUANS

a man should stand at six o'clock on a September morning. Where the shadow of his head fell, lay the buried gold.

Lebreau's grandson came next to look for the gold. He was drowned in the San Juan River. Neither maps nor papers were found on his body. But before he started on his ill-fated trip, he had left copies of both with a Frenchman who passed the papers on to William Yule, Archuleta County rancher.

In the early 1870's, Asa Poor of Summitville found a grave he thought was that of an Indian chief and opened it looking for relics.

It was empty.

Could this be the mock grave—the clue to the buried treasure?

He told Yule about it, and both men were sure they had at last come upon the true trail. They formed a partnership, included two other men in the deal, and located the empty grave without difficulty. To guard their secret, they destroyed anything that looked like a marking, dynamiting the trees blazed with peculiar signs. Then they set to work, fired by a hope and enthusiasm that died little by little, as no gold came to light. Divining rods, or "doodle-bugs," were used, but magnetic iron in the earth made them useless.

Several years later, Asa Poor hired a man with a mineral rod not affected by iron to locate gold in the earth. The rod indicated a spot some two miles from the false grave. Poor and his men dug down about four feet in the new location. Here was a walled shaft about twenty feet deep. Shaking with excitement—this was the spot for sure! —they lowered themselves down the shaft to examine it.

It was empty and bare as a bone.

Undismayed, they sank four other shafts to depths of forty-two to sixty-three feet around the central shaft. There was nothing but more dirt, more stubborn rock, and twisted roots of ancient trees. At last they admitted defeat, and quit the search.

The Archuletas spent nearly $50,000 in a fruitless earch.

Montroy, one of Poor's partners, had a copy of the map for several years. On his death it disappeared. He had believed implicitly in the map because of the many markings that were actually found as indicated. He also believed that the treasure was never found. Others think the second party of Frenchmen did find it and by some devious means got it back to their native land in secret. It is possible that the Indians or the Spaniards discovered it before the opening up of the San Juan country.

But it is most likely that the vast horde of millions in gold still lies in its deep, protected grave on a silent mountainside, high in the mighty San Juans.

Also told by Editha L. Watson in the *Central City Register-Call*, 1935; Ila P. Montroy in *Pioneers of the San Juan County*, Volume 1, 1942

SECTION 2-B

(See Frontispiece Map for Location)

Murdie's Lost Gold Mine

A gold-bearing vein, running $5,000 to the ton, was discovered suddenly and as suddenly lost.

It happened in Taylor Park in Gunnison County. Murdie, a locomotive machinist from Topeka, Kansas, used to take his vacation every summer in Gunnison for his favorite pastime, prospecting. One year on the last day of his vacation he stopped at a small bubbling creek. The water was so clear you could see the clean sand in its bed sketching swirling, shining patterns. You could see every pebble and rock, and the sun glinting on them made every one seem studded with diamonds and gold.

Murdie peered closer. That looked like an ore-bearing vein, some fifteen inches wide, in the bottom of the creek. With his pick he dug out a sample, packed it away, and next day went home to Topeka.

Sorting his specimens one night, the one from the creek bed looked richer than the others, and he decided to have it assayed. The report astounded him: gold, $5,000 to the ton!

Murdie was rich. Or would be as soon as he got back to that creek in Taylor Park next summer. But when he did return, neither he nor his son, W. D. Murdie (whose aid he enlisted), could find the place. Different water levels made it impossible to locate even the creek. The stream considered as most likely had no ore-bearing vein in its bed. Murdie finally gave up the search, having one good-looking specimen and one assayer's report to remind him mockingly how close he once was to being rich.

If ever that vein is discovered again, it will mean a real gold-rush to Gunnison County—for this vein is richer than that of the famed Lost Dutchman mine of the Superstition Mountains in Arizona.

Also told by the *Gunnison Courier*, 1950

Mysterious Gold of Juan Carlos

Juan Carlos, riding up from Taos into the San Luis Valley in 1860, was dark, arrogant and handsome, with a regal manner. He had a large number of peons, and the saddle of the horse he rode was weighed down with gleaming silver ornaments. His long pack train was loaded with such luxuries as books and paintings, with elegant Spanish hats and velvet attire for himself. He set up a home in the valley, where he ruled his household in a lordly way, demanding much service but paying for it generously—in gold dust.

The first of May each year Juan Carlos disappeared. Nobody knew why or where—he simply vanished. Many were the questions and wonderings—had he been killed, had he fled the country?—Then on the last day of October, he returned as mysteriously as he had left.

For three years this happened. The curiosity of the valley people mounted, but Don Carlos was not the sort of man you questioned. The fourth year some of the Spanish-Americans, either braver or more curious than the rest, hid all night near Carlos' home. When he left in the morning, by himself as usual, they followed furtively. They were not furtive enough. Carlos went only a short distance, turned around and came home. That year he did not make his mysterious journey.

About five years later—in 1868—Carlos hired several of the most ignorant Spanish-Americans he could find to build several large adobe houses on the shores of the San Luis Lakes. (These lakes are fifteen to twenty miles northeast of Alamosa.) He paid them generously with gold dust, and ordered them—all but two—never to step foot near the houses again if they wanted to live.

The two he ordered to stay with him were never seen again.

Their families went to Carlos to ask about them. They were met by Carlos' most arrogant, freezing disdain. The two had gone with the others. He had not seen them since the day he paid them their due wages.

The families knew that Carlos lied. He had had the unfortunate two do some secret work, then killed them to seal their lips. But what kind of work and what secret baffled the Spanish-Americans. It must have something to do with the haughty Spaniard's endless supply of gold.

Juan Carlos died as proudly and aloofly as he had lived. Within a year two Spanish-Americans in the valley suddenly bought large herds of sheep and cattle. They claimed they had made the money in government contract work near Santa Fe—a flimsy tale. Unskilled laborers who had made only a daily pittance all their lives did not suddenly make a fortune in contract work.

The houses near the lakes, used as late as 1885 by hunters, had the same air of mystery about them as their lordly owner. Although they were often searched, inch by inch, no secrets were found, no treasure maps, no notes or gold mines.

The source of the Spaniard's wealth has never been explained nor discovered. Some think an unknown explorer on his way to California may have found the hidden cache. Some think that the houses on the San Luis Lakes were merely a decoy. Actually Don Carlos was operating a placer high on the Alamosa River in the region of Jasper, Wightman Fork Creek, and Summitville where immensely rich gold deposits were found in 1870. Some think that the *Cavern of Skulls* (see accompanying story), which was some twenty odd miles northeast of his San Luis houses, was where Don Carlos secreted his gold. These same people think that the skulls belonged to those men that Don Carlos murdered.

Who knows now at this late date? Anyone of the three explanations has elements of logic. If the *Cavern of Skulls* was his, and a landslide did obscure the opening to his cave, then it is quite possible that the high Sangre de Cristos still hold a cave, laden with gold dust and gold bars.

Also told by Editha Watson in the *Liberty Press* (Denver), 1935

The Cavern of the Skulls

Human skulls and bars of solid gold in a remote mountain cavern comprise the dramatic elements of an adventure three snowbound prospectors stumbled into, back in October of 1880. At the head of Dead Man's Creek in the Sangre-de Cristo Range of Saguache County, several miles above Deadman Cow Camp, was the location of the cavern.

Three men—S. J. Harkman, E. R. Oliver and H. A. Melton—were prospecting in those loftly, picturesque mountains where legends of lost gold and Spanish treasure go back hundreds of years before our recorded Western history begins. On the San Luis Valley side, about two miles north of Dead Man's Creek, the prospectors were caught by a blizzard. They staggered about blindly for a time, all directions lost in the spinning snow and savage wind. Panic-stricken that they would never make it out of the storm alive, imagine their relief when they fell into a tunnel opening in the rocky side of the canyon! They did not worry what might be inside—to them it was shelter from the blizzard, and a life-saver.

They managed to find a few dry pines for torches under the ledge of the opening. Then they crawled on their hands and knees, single-file, through the narrow tunnel for ten or twelve feet. Suddenly they were in a large room where they could stand upright. Their torches cast eeries shadows all about them. Water dripped from the irregular roof of the cave. The air was heavy and cold with the dank, musty smell of inside the earth.

Melton, walking gingerly about the room, discovered an opening to another passage. With the eternal curiosity of the prospector they decided to see where it led. They had to proceed on hands and knees again. After some ten feet they emerged into a much deeper and larger chamber—so big, in fact, that their torches did not light up walls. Oliver, walking ahead, struck his foot against something that moved easily. He lowered his light.

The red flames of the torch lit up a human skull.

The prospectors stood in silent horror for a time. Harkman cleared his throat.

"There's four more," he said hoarsely, pointing.

Oliver rubbed his hands briskly. "Well, boys, don't know about you, but I'm freezing—and starving. Let's go back for wood and build a fire so we can eat."

They soon had a fire blazing in the cave peopled with human skulls. Turning their backs on their ghostly companions, they warmed up beans and biscuits and coffee and ate. And all the while they ate, the ghosts whispered. The silent white bones spoke. This strange hidden cave, the entrance so easily passed over in the side of the thickly timbered canyon, held a mysterious secret. A secret now guarded by death for who knew how many years.

After supper the men lighted new torches and explored further. Near one wall another skull and bones were found. But no tools, no guns or knives—nothing but decaying skeletons. Turning to the right, the prospectors found another passage which led them into a smaller chamber. Here the walls were much more irregular with huge projecting rocks, some of them shelf-like. Melton played his torch-light along the lower wall where a stone extended some ten inches from the floor like a long shelf. Under it were several large stones, oddly uniform in shape and size. Melton tried to lift one, and it was so heavy he could scarcely budge it. He yelled to the other two who came running.

The wavering light of the pine torches flashed on solid gold bars.

THE SANGRE DE CRISTOS HIDE SPANISH GOLD

In their excitement the men found it hard to wait out the storm before returning to camp with their treasure, worth thousands of dollars. By morning the blizzard had stopped, and shouldering their new riches, they made their way back to camp where they refused to tell the location of their find. There were more passages and more rooms they wanted to explore alone in their Cave of Bones. The five gold bars originally found were only an enticing promise of more hidden gold.

Storms and blizzards kept the prospectors from returning for several months. But the golden dreams of riches made the winter pass pleasantly. They knew exactly where to go—they had made mental notes and maps of the mysterious cave's opening. But when they got back, something had changed. This was surely the spot, they all agreed, but only bleak granite and earth sodden with spring snows faced them in the canyon wall.

They were possibly in the wrong gulch? Wrong canyon? After all, a blizzard had been raging when they stumbled into the tunnel mouth. Maybe—maybe. Years later they were still saying "Maybe." Maybe here—maybe there.

There are so many canyons, so many gulches, so many winding, endless trails and so many caverns (such as the known *Caverna del Oro* close by) that it is easy to become confused. The most plausible explanation of the three prospectors' failure to re-locate their tunnel is that a landslide covered up the opening.

The cave is probably still there, under the rock and earth—and the way to the narrow damp passages, the dark whispering room with its decaying bones, and the solid gold bars.

Also told by *The Fairplay Flume*, 1880; *Empire Magazine: The Denver Post*, 1957

Caverna del Oro of Marble Mountain

The vast slopes of Marble Mountain and Milwaukee Peak above Westcliffe in the Sangre de Cristo Range, where early Spanish explorers roamed, are marked with many openings to great caves, deep and dangerous to explore. Only those who know the perils of mountain caves—poison air, floods, cave-ins—and who are equipped to meet emergencies, should dare to penetrate them. The mysterious caverns, exciting and alluring though their secrets may be, should be left to expert spelunkers and mountain climbers.

One of the most famous is called Cavern of Gold, *Caverna del Oro*, on Marble Mountain southwest of Westcliffe. It is in an almost inaccessible spot.

In 1869, Capt. Elisha P. Horn, discoverer of Horn Peak, found a skeleton clad in Spanish armor, pierced by an Indian arrow, in the opening of *Caverna del Oro*. Below the cave are ruins of a fort, and along the mountainside the remains of rifle pits commanding a view of Wet Mountain Valley. Horn was very intrigued but came to no conclusion.

In 1932 Peter Moser of Denver reported that he had seen a skeleton chained to a rock in the cave. A seven-man party was organized to investigate. They reached the Maltese cross indicating the cavern entrance, only to find that dynamite blasts had closed off the opening. They found arrowheads scattered about, further proof that Indians once fought here, probably to rout Spanish gold seekers.

In the mid-1930's, members of the Colorado Mountain Club and the Historical Society descended vertically three hundred feet into the cave. They found evidences of ancient occupants—hoisting apparatus and ladders, crude hand-forged tools, rotting bones, and even rudely constructed living-rooms. A red Maltese cross, chiseled in a rock, marks the entrance to the cavern.

It is said that seven hundred feet down are two huge oaken doors, and that these guard mines or storehouses for Spanish gold. On the slope of the mountain, at about the same level as the doors, is an old log and stone building. It is believed a tunnel leads from this to the storehouse inside the mountain.

There is little doubt that this cave and others were places of refuge for early Spanish settlers, and no doubt that they were gold miners. If, as so often happened, they were forced to flee suddenly from attacking Indians, there may still be a cache of gold buried somewhere in any of the half dozen caves on Marble Mountain.

Also told by the *Summit County Journal* (Breckenridge), 1936; *Rocky Mountain News*, 1955

(See Frontispiece Map for Location)

Letter in the Wallet

In the gold-rush days anxious families waited long and fearfully in their Eastern homes for news of the hardy souls who braved the long dangerous journey across the plains in pursuit of riches. Letters took months to reach their destination. Some never arrived at all because of Indian raids, floods, blizzards and sudden death.

Bill Skinner was one of those who waited in vain in his Illinois home for news from his brother George. Finally he went West himself, determined to learn if his brother lived or died.

He found his first clue in Denver (formerly Denver City). A grocer remembered George very well and said:

"He was here in '63, eight years ago. He loaded up on supplies, paid for them and left me a couple hundred dollars to keep for him until he got back, saying he was headed for the gulches in the Sangre de Cristos. He never came back."

Skinner traveled to the Wet Mounutain Valley at the foot of the Sangre de Cristo range where he made friends with the ranchers in hopes they knew something about George. One remembered a red-headed young man by the name of Skinner.

"Yep, he went through here, but he didn't stay long—he was mighty anxious to hit the diggings. Never seen him since," was the answer.

Others remembered a sandy-haired George, and a bald one, and a drunken black-haired prospector who swore he would never turn up again unless he brought ten thousand in gold on his back. That did not sound like George, a serious, quiet young man whose hair was an ordinary brown.

Thousands of prospectors came and went through the valley. It was no wonder a peaceful, sober young fellow went unnoticed and unremembered. Skinner hired a guide and spent the summer searching the mountains—an endless, hopeless task. He found leads as confusing and conflicting as the ranchers had given him. He followed through on every one faithfully, but without success.

Suddenly a weird chain of coincidences made a strangle-hold on his credulity—yet no stranger than many of the things which happened in the wild and fabulous West. Skinner and the guide, ready to abandon the search with winter coming on, camped one night at timberline on the eastern slope of Horn's Peak. Nearby was an old log cabin, its windowless walls sagging and weather-beaten, its dirt roof ready to cave in.

Skinner went inside and found the usual small square room with earth floor, rotting plank table and three-legged stool, rusted tin stove, chimney stuck through a hole in the wall. Sticking out from a mud-chinked log not far from the chimney, he saw an old leather wallet, wound around with wire. He stuck it in his pocket to examine later, as the guide was yelling at him they had better get started—those black clouds hanging below the peak meant snow.

When Skinner later examined the wallet, merely out of curiosity, he found a letter from his brother George! Written only six months after he left Illinois, George said he had made his strike—a rich one. He was now heading for the settlements, to spend the winter and get outfitted for the return trip in the spring, when he would develop his mine. Just in case something happened to him, he wanted his brother to have the mine. He was writing this letter, giving the location of his find and asking the finder to notify his brother in Illinois.

Skinner could hardly believe his senses. Just when he had given up all hope, to stumble on the one real clue, the most important one yet! He kept his story to himself, and in the spring hired the same guide again. Skinner said he wanted to start the search where it had been broken off in the fall, at the old cabin on Horn's Peak.

A mile or so before they reached the location, they could see the cruel forces of nature had been at work during the winter, changing everything. Snowslides had torn off the face of the slope; where a gulch had been was now a mountain. Trees, boulders—and cabin—were gone, ground into dust at the foot of the hill.

Refusing to give up, Skinner kept on looking, hoping both for some other sign of his brother as well as for the mine. The directions in the letter were worthless after the slide, for George had used the cabin and certain trees near it, also a spire-shaped granite boulder, as a starting-point.

October came too soon. Skinner had to end the search until next year. Going down, the trail threaded along the vast, flat face of a great precipice, and their burros, cautious and sure-footed by nature, moved slowly. The uncertain trail gave way in places, and they hung out over space for terrifying moments. Rocks dislodged by the small hooves clattered down, echoing and re-echoing far below. Above loomed the grim high peaks, and the autumn wind blew endlessly through the scraggly timberline trees.

Suddenly one of the pack burros slipped and fell, rolling down in a cloud of dust to the depths below. Skinner and the guide managed to clamber down the cliff in order to retrieve the pack—the burro, of course, was killed in the fall. Near their dead animal, they saw two skeletons, one of a man and the other of a burro, dead for years. A leather bag, cracked and storm-bitten but still whole, lay a little distance away. The camping outfit, packed on the burro's back, lay strewn beside the animal, and in it a small fortune in gold dust. The man's death had clearly been accidental—a solitary death on a remote mountain precipice —and he had lain, with his gold, without discovery until now.

It was here the chain of coincidence tightened to such a point Skinner was dizzy. Or was it, as he liked to believe, the gentle spirit of his brother reaching across the sky spaces to help him? For in the leather bag, preserved all these years, was a diary by George Skinner. He wrote about the wallet he had left in the cabin, and how he hoped it would eventually get to his brother in case he never returned. He was well aware how dangerous these lonely mountains were, and how possible it was he would never return from his mine with the gold he had found. His mine, he wrote, was enough to blind a body. The gold stuck right out of the rock, lots of it so loose and crumbly that it could be picked off with the bare hands.

For nine years, the bones and diary and gold of George Skinner had lain bleaching on the mountainside, waiting to be found. Skinner sadly buried the bones where they lay, and returned to Illinois. The following spring he returned to the mountains to search for his brother's rich strike.

But in vain—maybe George had been able to direct his brother to his body. After that, his ghostly power vanished.

To this day, not that mine, nor any approaching such richness, has ever been found in those gulches. The snowslides cruel whimsy, obliterating one man's feeble attempt against the mountain's inexorable might, did its work well. Its secret is still not known.

Also told by Editha L. Watson in the *Herald Democrat* (Leadville), 1935

The Phantom Auto

Sometimes the spirits who guard buried treasure do not want that treasure discovered, and they take weird and mystic means to prevent it. The ghosts of the old prospectors rise up in wrath to frighten away the looters who would desecrate their treasure-graves.

There are many such tales. One of the most unusual, which is still fresh in the minds of the people living in San Pedro in Costilla County, is the story of the phantom automobile. Surely there is no reason why a ghost should not use a modern invention like the automobile. In this case it proved to be a strong and effective weapon.

The legends of buried treasure in the beautiful Sangre de Cristo Range of southern Colorado are numerous. Many are based on genuine records, handed down from generation to generation, just as stories of phantoms guarding these treasures have come down from one age to another.

In Central City we have the tommy-knockers, genial little imps who used to warn the Cornish miners of dangers in the shafts and tunnels. Today the tommy-knockers might decide to warn intruders to get out of the mines of those workers they were loyal to long ago. In the Southwest there are old crones with hypnotic, ever-youthful eyes or mad dogs that vanish as they bark or invisible rattlesnakes with a loud rattle or tiny nude girls of enchanting beauty—little creatures with perfect bodies, hair of rippling gold and starry blue eyes. They all might band together in the spirit-world to keep the wrong people from finding gold.

Four men from the San Luis Valley decided to work on one group of spirits—the tiny, beautiful fairy women said to haunt the trout streams in the summer time. If a fisherman saw one of these and had the courage to follow, she would lead him to one of the vast buried treasures hidden in a landslide in the nearby Sangre de Cristo mountains.

~~~~~~

Jesse James' Loot

Half Moon Gulch, shown on the opposite page, was the hang-out of the notorious bandit's gang during 1879 and was commented upon in the Leadville Chronicle *of that year. Although no definite robberies in Colorado were ascribed to them, they were known to be in various upper Arkansas River towns during the following years. Frank James and other members of the gang registered in 1883 at the Hotel Jackson in Poncha Springs where their signatures may still be seen. Old-timers of Lake County believe they cached loot in this gulch and that they never returned for all of it. Half Moon Gulch is in Section 2-A of Colorado.*

41

The four fishermen spent several summers without glimpsing a nude golden-haired fairy, but one did discover in an abandoned shack a map of a secret mine. The directions were so clear that they decided, since the little ladies were paying them no heed, to go out on their own. Very secretive about their preparations, they slipped out of town one moonless night.

Making sure they were not followed, they headed into the mountains, going east and north. They had studied the map so thoroughly that they knew every turn in the winding gulch, and they recognized certain signs, like the stone profile of an old Indian chief minus his headdress, outlined against the starry sky by a jutting precipice. Fifty paces north of the stone face they turned to the right and counted fifty paces up the slope. Here, as the map said, was a steep cliff running along the top of the canyon which lay from east to west. Halfway up this cliff the treasure was buried.

The men were shaking, not from fatigue, but with awe and excitement. The map was perfect! Everything fell into place exactly as the faded notations on the yellowed bit of paper said. They lit a lantern and started digging. Fired by enthusiasm, it did not take them long to hammer through the stubborn rock-studded earth, making a deep, wide-mouthed hole.

Suddenly one of the men stood erect, wiping his perspiring forehead with the back of his hand. He scowled as a small shiver scudded through him.

"Funny thing," he whispered. "Minute ago, the wind was howling. Now—listen—it's so quiet—so blamed quiet—not a sound!"

The others joined him, peering up at the great pine and *pinon* trees above them, cutting out the starry sky.

"It's dark and thick as tar," one muttered, just as a voice, shrill with fury, yelled a string of curses from the black void. Next instant a stooped giant in ten-gallon hat, sheepskin coat and high boots, stepped into the circle of yellow light cast by the lantern.

"Get out of here!" he thundered. "I'm deputy sheriff, and you can't dig here. This is private property."

The four men froze. Only one could find his voice.

"You ain't no deputy sheriff!" he blustered. "I know every single one in every town in the whole valley. And this ain't private property either!"

The giant's deep-set, burning eyes glared at the speaker. He raised his arm as if to strike him. But instead he turned and left the circle of light. The miners let out their breath. They never said a word. They rolled cigarettes and smoked a minute. Whoever the huge stranger was, he had been mad enough to kill, and yet he had stalked off without a word.

The fingers holding the cigarettes were not quite steady. But hearing no further sounds, the men went back to work. According to the map, they were not far from the hidden gold. Two of the men went down in the hole to dig, while the other two shoveled dirt and rocks from the mouth of the excavation.

Suddenly in the quiet night air came the sound of a car door being slammed, then a starter grinding away, followed by the roaring of a motor. The two men in the hole leaped out to stand gulping at the other two, who also gulped. They had heard it—all four of them—yet there was no highway within fifteen miles. No car could possibly get up the steep, rocky, winding gulch trail. But they heard the car, and now powerful twin headlights flashed through the trees, and the car was coming nearer, nearer—crashing through brush, slamming against boulders. The four, rooted to the spot in stark astonishment, were blinded by the lights as the car came racing straight at them, lurching and swinging on the thin rocky ledge. Wild panic sent the four jumping as one into the hole where they covered their heads in terror.

The automobile came on—passed over them—roared off into the night.

It was some time before the men, paralyzed with fear, could move. But eventually, as there was no sound in the night except the wind rattling the branches above, they clambered out and looked for signs of the car.

There were none. Not so much as the faintest tire mark.

They looked at the almost perpendicular cliff the car had raced up, and the equally steep precipice on which it had vanished.

Without a word they picked up their tools and strode down the mountainside.

Somewhere on a ledge not too far from San Pedro is a buried treasure of great wealth. Dancing around it in the moonlight are half a dozen tiny, beautiful figures of nude women with long golden hair. Their tinkling, nectar-sweet laughs echo teasingly through the dark gulches. Whoever is brave enough to risk meeting a phantom sheriff and his phantom car may see them for a minute or two while the night becomes very still, so still that even the wind hushes its endless moaning through the high *pinon* trees.

Also told by William Wallrich in *Empire Magazine: The Denver Post*, 1956

Arapaho Princess Treasure

The romance of an Arapaho Princess and a dashing Spaniard is the heart of one of the most persistent legends of buried Spanish gold. He was the leader of a small band working in the foothills near the Spanish Peaks west of what is now Walsenburg. There in the 1800's, the prospectors had made a rich strike.

The Spanish settled by to work their mine which continued to pour out high-grade ore. Most of their wealth was sent home to Spain with the hope that they could all retire to the life of a grandee. As the mine grew bigger, they needed help and hired some Arapaho Indians.

The leader of the Spaniards fell in love with the daughter of the chief, a proud and willowy black-eyed girl of flashing beauty. In due time they were married, and the story of their marriage is warm and tender—the Indian Princess' adoring love, and the Spaniard's ardent devotion. A baby daughter completed their happiness. Gold from the mine kept the family in what luxuries and comfort could be found in the far-off West where as yet only trappers, Indians and Spanish explorers lived.

After several years an uprising by the neighboring Utes, determined to wipe out the white men, shattered the little paradise of the princess and her husband. The Arapaho chief advised his son-in-law and the other white men to leave until the Utes had quieted down. The Spaniards agreed this was good advice.

They loaded their gold in fifty-pound bars on a burro train and were ready to leave when word came that the Utes were near. In order to escape, they would have to travel faster than a burro train could move, so they buried their gold in a place marked by a great rock standing thirty feet high. In certain light the rock looked like a giant doll, and the Spaniards named it La Muneca.

The delay in hiding their gold cost all but two of them, the leader and a companion, their lives. Both fled to Santa Fe, and from there to Spain.

But the Spaniard could not forget his Indian princess. For ten long years he yearned for her. Finally he was able to make the trip back to the Spanish Peaks. His eagerness to see his wife and daughter—who would be thirteen years old now—made the trip endless. Alas, when after many months of journeying, he reached home, it was to find that his princess had died. Heartbroken, he had no interest in the gold that he and his men had buried, and he refused to talk about it. It was, somehow, the cause of his sorrow; it had, somehow, cost him his beloved wife.

His daughter grew up and married, but the Spaniard still grieved for his wife. Becoming ill and knowing death was near, he told his daughter and her husband where the gold was hidden. But he warned them it was cursed—it would bring only sorrow to anyone coveting it.

The daughter and her husband never touched the hidden treasure nor told anyone its location. At length when she was old and alone, her husband dead, and her sons begging her to reveal the riches they could so well use, she reluctantly made a promise. When the snow cleared in the spring, she would tell the secret.

As the snows began to run in rivulets, the Indian Princess became very ill. Just before she died, she called her sons and told them that the gold lay near La Muneca. The sign was a small rock in the shape of a niche in which lay an old iron shovel. Under that rock lay the gold.

Her sons immediately set out to find the rock with the spade. La Muneca was not hard to find—it was a landmark for miles—but the niche-like rock with the old iron shovel—where was it? Every possible stone and boulder were examined, and every foot of ground near La Muneca.

A neighbor, passing by, wondered what his friends were doing and stopped to chat. He mentioned casually that last fall he had been hunting deer right about here, and had found an old shovel on one of the rocks. He had used the shovel to clear away snow from the camp site.

Stunned, the princess' sons stared in bitter disappointment. Finally one found his voice and asked if he knew on what stone he had found the spade. The neighbor shook his head, gesturing with his arms to include the miles and miles stretching beyond La Muneca.

"One rock—out of all those? A million or so out there, don't you think?" He gave them a baffled look. "What difference does it make? An old shovel on an old rock!"

The sons of the Indian Princess made no answer.

Many treasure hunters have dug under countless rocks near La Muneca in the Spanish Peaks. No one has found the long-ago fortune of the unfortunate Spaniards. It remains buried—until a lucky searcher may, some day, find his spade stopped by something hard in that earth. The something hard may turn out to be a bar of gold.

Also told by the *Rocky Mountain News,* 1959

PIKES PEAK HIDES BURCH'S RICH GOLD MINE

Prospector's Return

One balmy September day, in 1948, the Colorado Springs police received a letter from Mae McGrath in Denver, asking them to search for her uncle, a ninety-year-old prospector.

The prospector's undying faith is a legend more true than the trails of buried treasure he has left behind him. William Burch of Wabasso, Florida, was no exception to the rule. His faith remained unwavering and bright through half a century.

Burch left his wife and home in the 1890's to prospect in the area on which lofty Pikes Peak looks down indifferently on world-famous Cripple Creek and Victor.

Burch was about five feet, seven inches tall, with squinting blue eyes that searched constantly for the strike that would send him home a rich and triumphant man. Like so many prospectors, he preferred to work alone, trekking off every morning at dawn into the tangled maze of gulches and canyons making up the ore-rich terrain. Just where he went and what he was finding, he kept to himself. His wiry figure, a familiar sight in Victor, Colorado, seemed tireless. The white head of Pikes Peak, sentinel of the plains and guardian of some of the richest gold discoveries in history, was his landmark. Usually he was noticed heading for its south slope, ten or fifteen miles from Victor.

After several years of prospecting there was a change in Burch—something a little cocky in his walk, something a little brighter in his eyes. The Victor miners, fond of the mild little man, teased him about striking it rich and hiding his loot.

Burch only smiled with the smugness of a man who could talk if he wanted to—and didn't want to. Only once or twice did he make what might be considered a slip or two. Putting these bits of conversation together, the old-time miners decided Burch had discovered a vein of rich ore. Rumors, in the way they have, grew. Burch had a mine like the famous Strong mine of Victor. Burch had made one of the richest discoveries in the whole district. Burch's mine was a tunnel with walls of solid gold. The mild blue-eyed man was a figure of mystery with the fame and stature mystery imparts.

At the very height of the excitement Burch disappeared.

Foul play was suspected, and many a search organized. But neither Burch nor any evidence of his diggings, was found. Then his landlady said he had struck it rich and retired. As one exciting event after the other happened in the normal course of life in Colorado's lushest gold camp, the quiet man was forgotten.

But Burch himself, whatever the reason for his disappearance and whatever he did in the intervening years, did not forget his mine on the south slope of Pikes Peak. His faith in its riches, were they real or just the product of a prospector's shining faith, never died.

In 1948 he left his home in Florida, saying he planned to return to a rich mine he had owned years ago. He passed through Denver to see his niece and then disappeared. The woman was worried, as her uncle was ninety-years old and feeble.

The white-haired old man was found wandering on the south side of Pikes Peak, about fifteen miles from Victor. He died soon after without revealing where his mine was—if indeed he had found it again. His secret died with him; but prospectors near Pikes Peak are still keeping an eye open for a long-abandoned mine that is just as rich, or richer, than the Strong Mine of Victor.

Also told by the *Rocky Mountain News,* 1948

Treasure in Trinchera Creek

A paymaster was driving to Fort Garland with an iron-bound chest containing the bi-yearly payroll for the soldiers. He dreamed of the trout fishing he would get back to in the morning. There was nothing like fishing to while away the boring hours at the fort—things were quiet, the Indians behaving, and outlaws lying low for a change. Not very far from here, he thought, as the cumbersome old ambulance rattled along the rocky road bordering Trinchera Creek, was his favorite fishing-hole. Once he got safely inside the walls of the fort with the gold that meant so much to the waiting soldiers, he would be back here—fishing to his heart's content.

His fond dreams were destined never to come true.

Fort Garland, situated in the San Luis Valley of southern Colorado, helped to guard the country from unfriendly Utes and Apaches in the early days of the West. When the Indians were quiet, there was little for the soldiers to do but dream of adventure, or the women they had left behind. As time dragged, they turned each in his own way to something that would relieve the day-in-day-out boredom of the lonely fort in the Sangre de Cristo wilderness. Some drank, some gambled, some fought, and some—including the paymaster—fished for trout in the clear mountain streams.

Twice a year the paymaster drove to Fort Union in New Mexico in a horse-drawn ambulance with a guard of four mounted soldiers to draw the payroll—several thousand dollars—for the men and officers of Fort Garland. This was his spring trip. He had arrived safely in Fort Union, picked up the chest with the gold, and started homeward. He had to be more watchful on the trip home just in case some greedy outlaws, knowing his route, lay in wait. But he knew the four mounted guards were also keeping a sharp lookout. The wagon rocketed at top speed down the sharp grade of Trinchera Creek. The paymaster noted they were already at Gray Back Gulch which was within a few miles of Fort Garland and only a mile or so from his favorite fishing-hole.

A barrage of shots exploded in the clear mountain air. Three of the guards dropped as one man from their saddles, their bodies ripped by outlaw bullets. The fourth, leaping behind a boulder, held the two highwaymen at bay for a time. Finally he fell back, wounded. He was later found by the soldiers and was able to tell what had happened before he died.

In the meantime the team, terrified by the gun shots, panicked and fled pell-mell down the narrow, rocky road alongside the creek. The paymaster fell back in the wagon, feeling the warm trickle of blood on his head. By a tremendous effort he lifted the iron-bound box, heavy with gold. Despite the wild lurching of the wagon, he managed to crawl back up on the seat. He waited, blurred eyes searching the stream he had fished so often. He was waiting for that one spot—his favorite fishing-hole—a deep pool he knew well. Here the gold would be safe until soldiers from the fort could get it out.

Finally, where the road curved in closely to the creek, he saw it. With a last desperate effort the dying man shoved the chest from the speeding wagon and watched it land in the center of the pool.

The lookout at the fort had spotted the runaway ambulance by then. He immediately sent help, and the soldiers stopped the horses. Only after leading the horses inside the fort, did they discover the paymaster lying wounded in the back of the wagon.

"My favorite fishing-hole," the paymaster gasped. "Threw—box—favorite fishing-hole—ask my friends—"

They were his last words.

After burial had been provided for the courageous paymaster and his four guards, others—considered the best friends of the paymaster—were dispatched to get the paychest from the creek. They went to what one claimed was his favorite fishing-hole—the paymaster had showed it to him often.

The water was clear and shining above its bed of smooth empty sand. The men were baffled.

"But this was not his favorite fishing-hole," spoke up another of the soldiers. "Not the one he showed me—it's down around that bend."

The same empty pool mocked them there. Another spoke up.

"You're all wrong. He showed me the place—hundred yards from here. I'll show you."

Nothing in that silvery pool either.

One by one the soldiers insisted that they knew the paymaster's favorite fishing-hole. One by one the pools were examined—and found to be empty.

The iron-bound chest has never been recovered. Deep in the tumbling torrent of Trinchera Creek in the Sangre de Cristos just north of the New Mexico line, a fortune lies in a deep pool that was the brave paymaster's favorite fishing-hole. It may take another fisherman as good as he was to find it.

Also told by William Wallrich in *Empire Magazine: The Denver Post*, 1950; *Central City Register-Call*, 1954

48

(See Frontispiece Map for Location)

Treasure of the Strange Wagon

In the 1830's a black wagon, like a spring wagon, and six dead-black horses were seen on several moonlight nights, lunging below the huge tan, red and grey cliffs of the Purgatoire River, which flows into the Arkansas River a few miles below Bent's Fort. It was driven, so they say, by a Spaniard, carrying treasure. The driver himself was never seen except as a shadowy figure manipulating the reins of his flashing, struggling team. There were those who said he always wore light gloves—strange gloves that gleamed with a phosphorescent glow.

Where he came from, and where he went, remains a mystery. The only clues to his actual existence are some scattered thin gold ingots, crudely retorted, found in one of the caves that dot the grotesque sandstone cliffs. And a piece of harness, expensively made of finest leather and beautifully embossed in delicate designs with sterling silver.

Before gold was the lure to the West, there was beaver. As early as 1811, we have records of trappers in search of furs at the headwaters of the South Platte and Arkansas rivers. Unlike the prospector, who was afraid to trust anyone when it came to a rich strike, the trappers got together and talked. No doubt these early mountain men talked, among other things, about gold deposits.

Tales of Spanish explorers and their rich finds filtered through the deep forests and tangled gulches where they trapped beaver for silken pelts, killed buffalo for warm robes and bear for winter-proof coats. All these commodities were in demand in Eastern markets, even Europe. The mountain men were busy at their trade, and were a different breed from the later prospector whose gaze was glued to the earth, hoping for the glitter of pay ore.

But they heard tales, the mountain men, and they wondered. Often they gathered in the largest and most famous fort of the early West, built in 1832 by the two Bent brothers and Ceran St. Vrain, fur traders. Bent's Fort became a stopover for wagon trains hauling freight to Santa Fe, for exploration parties like the 1848 Fremont expedition, and for famous trappers like Kit Carson. Not much went on in the wide valley nor the high peaks that was not discussed in Bent's Fort.

We have no records that the trappers themselves tried to find out about the dark driver of the mysterious wagon-and-six. But the tales grew, augmented by words here and there around the Fort and from the Indians.

Years later the mountain men all but disappeared. Because of the scarcity of fur animals in the mountains and the diminishing demand for beaver and buffalo products—the vogue in the East now being for silk hats for men and sealskin coats for the ladies—trade fell off. They were replaced by wandering prospectors who appeared in Colorado after the discovery of gold in California in 1849.

These new men not only heard the story of the wagon and its gloved driver, but they found evidences that once a real wagon had traveled that rugged country, probably loaded with gold which was hidden in some of the deep caverns nearby. Stolen loot possibly, to be recovered when the bandit no longer feared detection. Or—as so often happened—simply a safe hiding place for the gold an honest miner had found many miles away, and planned to take home with him when conditions were right.

Whatever the real explanation of the wagon, it did pass up the Purgatoire Canyon below those vast cliffs many times. It vanished and then, after an interval sometimes long, sometimes short, the wagon headed into the south. In one cave a searcher found some Spanish tiles, traces of an ancient camp-fire, and a small iron-bound chest. The finder's high hopes were dashed when, broken open, it was empty except for a few thick gold coins. In a niche formed by a rock, some distance below the cave, he found the piece of harness, gleaming with expertly carved solid silver.

The man marked the place by thrusting two hunting-knives, one foot apart, in an ancient towering cottonwood tree, hoping to return and explore further. Then he saw another cave opening some distance away, which he might as well look into right now. Clambering toward it, he fell and broke his leg. He managed to climb toward the top of the cliff, where he lay for two days and nights before he was found, unconscious. He rallied enough to gasp out his story before he died. Others tried to find the two knives in the cottonwood, but the blade-pierced tree had, it seemed, given up the ghost and vanished in thin air.

Who was the intrepid driver with the six tar-black horses, their long manes flying through the night, while his skilled hands, in gloves that shone with a self-luminous radiance, guided them to a hidden cave in the Purgatoire Canyon? What happened to the treasure he undoubtedly carried? Is it still there, where he buried it?

The story goes that the old-timers are certain of one thing: the last trip made by the driver was a one-way trip. He arrived at the cliffs one moonlight night, but he never left. Whatever he had with him is still hidden somewhere in those strange sandstone cliffs above the Purgatoire River, a dozen or more miles from old Bent's Fort, later called Fort Lyon and a few miles northeast of the city of Las Animas.